THE
SUICIDE'S SON

A Story of Loss, Struggle and Hope

THE
SUICIDE'S SON

A Story of Loss, Struggle and Hope

JIM WOOTEN

GRANT & LEE
PUBLISHING

Greenville, South Carolina

The Suicide's Son: A Story of Loss, Struggle and Hope

ISBN 978-0-578-32269-8

Grant & Lee Publishing

Greenville, South Carolina

PUBLISHED IN THE UNITED STATES OF AMERICA

TO MY FATHER

"For thousands of years, father and son have stretched wistful hands across the canyon of time." — Alan Valentine

ACKNOWLEDGMENTS

For years, maybe decades, this book has been in my head. It only came to be written through the encouragement, support and assistance of more people than I could possibly mention, but I will try.

Chief among them, of course, is my wife, Becky, who has mastered the unenviable task of navigating the ever-changing currents of journeying through life with someone like me. In this project, when inspiration was flowing like a river, she urged me to ride it — to write and explore — and see where it took me, and she reveled in the discoveries along with me. In those stretches where doubt about the value of the effort and sadness in reliving some of the memories led into the shallows, she counseled patience and promised I would catch the current again. When the rapids threatened to overturn me, with so many details to take care of, she got in the boat with me — digging around for pictures I had misplaced, going to libraries and churches and interviews, editing and re-editing drafts before I let anyone else see them, advising, reassuring. I never would have reached shore without her.

I was concerned, because of the highly personal nature of the story and the stigma that is still too often attached to suicide, that my two children would be a little skittish about my publishing it, even though they never knew my father (or my mother, for that matter). I was grateful when both offered their support. My son jokingly said, "Just change my name to Billy if you talk about me." I guess you'll have to read a little further to find out their real names.

I owe a special debt of gratitude to those who shared their memories of my parents, and of the events that I sought to recount. After all this time, there were not many who could remember back that far, but the ones who did provided so much confidence for me in completing the story. For the most part, I did not name them at specific points, out of respect for their privacy, but their contribution was invaluable to me in confirming my own memories and fleshing out details. I am particularly indebted to Ed and Ruth Armstrong, longtime friends of my parents, whose recollections enriched the story incalculably. After letting them read the manuscript, I told them I would really like to acknowledge them if they were okay with it, and they graciously agreed.

I extend a special word of gratitude to Renee Howell, my only remaining cousin and therefore my closest remaining relative. Early on, my conversations with her and her enthusiastic insistence that I needed to complete this venture were pivotal in propelling me forward. She, more than anyone, shares the childhood memories I have of growing up in our family.

To Phillip and Wendi Lynn, for the Fripp Island retreat in which the first pages were written; to the staff of both the Laurens County Library and the Laurens County Museum, for help in historical research; to attorney Reid Cox and the congregation of the Church of the Epiphany, for researching church records; to Jim Watson, who took some time to really listen to an old childhood buddy — all of you played a vital role in helping me tell my story. I thank you all. To those who took a first look at the book and offered helpful feedback — my sisters-in-law Lew and Lyn Brabham, brother-in-law Dan Simon, ministry colleague Stephen Clyborne, and Laurens native and friend Herbert Adams — thank you for the encouragement and guidance.

Once I wrote the book, I had no idea how to publish it — or whether I should even try. Enter one Butch Blume! He had helped a couple of friends in a similar endeavor, and graciously agreed to advise me. He did more than that! Along with his expertise, he offered "a word, fitly spoken" that gave me the courage to move ahead and step out in faith and in the hope that these words may be a help to someone else who is walking a similar path that I have walked. My thanks, dear friend! I would never have made it through the jungle of publishing without you as my guide.

And finally, my sincere appreciation to Denise Huffman, who prepared the manuscript for publication, serving as the copy editor and formatter; again, to Butch Blume, who designed the book cover; and to the folks at IngramSpark, who put it all together into the printed edition you hold in your hand. I have learned that the act of "writing" a book is much more than a solitary figure putting words and thoughts to paper. It is truly a collaboration.

CONTENTS

PREFACE

The last time I saw my father alive was on Father's Day, 1962. I was ten years old, an only child, fresh out of the fourth grade. While the passing of fifty-nine birthdays since makes the sequence of events a little uncertain in my mind, the scenes themselves are burned into my memory in vivid detail.

Do you know how you can call up certain segments of a favorite movie that you have watched time and again — describe the setting, recite the dialogue, relive the emotions you felt when you first saw it? The events surrounding that fateful and pivotal weekend in my life, like snippets from a movie I wish I had never seen, are like that for me. Without warning — with some trigger, some word, some encounter, some feeling in the air — they pop into my consciousness again. It is as if someone hits the "play" button, and the scenes roll across some inner screen one more time, whether I want them to or not.

Jumbled emotions crowd together when I think of my father, long gone. Maybe that is the case for all of us, but certainly when a suicide is involved. The words that follow on these pages are an attempt (long overdue) to "un-jumble," as much as is possible, some of those emotions. In that sense, this book began as a highly personal quest to discover a measure of peace by finding a more coherent narrative of my father's death and a fuller appreciation of his life.

Is such a quest even possible? Emotionally, can you ever recapture the good times and the richness of the relationship, unsullied by the memory of how the relationship ended? Do the good qualities of the person get lost, considering the definitive act of his or her life? How does one honestly confront the failings that lead to such an action and yet not lose the breadth of the person who was beloved? It is no easy task, but the act of writing has helped. Putting thoughts and memories to paper has at least moved me further down the road toward peace, toward coherency, and even toward a rediscovery of who my father was to me, beyond the grave hurt his death brought to me.

Outside that somewhat therapeutic goal (daunting as it may be) lies the desire that, in sharing my story, others whose lives have been touched by suicide would find comfort in being reminded that they are not alone in the tangled emotions and unresolved questions that comprise their own loss. Suicide is such a staggering reality with which to deal. It is incomprehensible. It can never be explained satisfactorily. You want to ask the only one who could possibly answer your questions, and he (or she) is gone. And even if they were here, could they even explain it? I doubt it. Explanations are rational. Suicide is not. It seems so unnatural and so painful that (at least in my experience) few, if any, of those left behind opt to speak of it.

As a minister, only when I have dared to publicly refer to my experience, usually in a sermon, has someone sought me out, away from the crowd, and whispered, "You know, I lost someone like that, too." Sometimes, haltingly, they share bits of their story — who, when, sometimes how, seldom in tremendous detail. Mostly, they just want me to know they share the bond of the unspeakable. I have been continually surprised at how many lives have been touched by suicide — because, by and large, it is not talked about.

Lauren Oliver describes it well: "Suicide. A sideways word, a word that people whisper and mutter and cough; a word that must be squeezed out behind cupped palms or murmured behind closed doors."[1]

With this book, I choose not to whisper or mutter or cough, but to speak as openly as I am able of my father's suicide, and of the impact I perceive it has had upon me. It is not easy to do so. For one thing, because it is so personal, I find myself asking, "Is the sharing of this story somehow a betrayal of my father, and others whose lives were entwined with his?" I hope not. Instead, I trust that those who read these pages will share my affection for the very real, extraordinarily complex people of whom I write. Silence is no longer an option.

In her most helpful volume, *Night Falls Fast: Understanding Suicide*, Kay Redfield Jamison, a professor at the Johns Hopkins School of Medicine, points to the challenge of speaking or writing about a particular suicide: "Each way to suicide is its own: intensely private, unknowable, and terrible. Suicide will seem to its perpetrator the last and best of bad possibilities, and any attempt by the living to chart the final terrain of life can be only a sketch, maddeningly incomplete."[2]

The story of any suicide is complex. One does not arrive at such a decision without a complicated back story. My father was no exception. The first part of the book recounts my memory of my father's life — and his death — but as Jamison says, all I can offer is "a sketch, maddeningly incomplete." I wish I would have written it earlier. In some ways, I may have waited too late. My father would be ninety-five this year, if he had lived — so almost all his contemporaries are gone. (Amazingly, I discovered and reconnected with some, including one couple whose friendship with my parents was deep and reached beyond the time of their courtship.) Even when others were alive, they were not prone to talk about him, or especially the particulars of his death and the circumstances that surrounded it. I think they were afraid to broach the subject with me — and I was afraid to address the subject with them.

Still, most of my memories are clear, and I have clung to every morsel of information shared with me down through the years. Though I look back through the lens of a ten-year-old, those memories have been refined by the insights and experiences of decades of living.

In voicing the second part of the story, I try to capture and better understand the perceived impact my father's suicide has had upon my own life. I do so with the aspiration that others who have been touched by suicide will, at the least, find comfort from knowing they are not alone in their struggles. Even better, I dare to hope that, for some, the courage to face the unsettled feelings they carry with them will awaken — enabling them to move forward in life with renewed resolve, despite the wounds they bear. Telling this part of the story presents challenges of its own. In many ways, trying to decipher the impact suicide has had upon my life confronts as much a mystery as trying to understand my father's actions.

How well does anyone really understand themselves? How

clearly do we recognize or acknowledge either the strengths or flaws within us? Would I have had the same insecurities, the same personality, the same experiences of faith, the same perceptions of God if my father had lived? I do not think so. I believe his death shaped my life and made me a different person, for better or worse, than if he had lived.

This is his story … and mine.

THE
SUICIDE'S SON

A Story of Loss, Struggle and Hope

Part I

Jim: Anatomy of a Suicide

Chapter 1

June 18, 1962: A Flash in the Night

He looked in the mirror as he prepared to go. He did not look so good. His jet-black hair, normally neatly coiffed, was downright shaggy. His distinctive hazel eyes did not gleam as they once had. They looked tired, sallow. He had liked it when people used to call him "Frankie" because of his resemblance to the young version of Sinatra (about 5'7", same smile, same facial structure); not so much when they called him "Spike" because they said he looked like the skeletal band leader Spike Jones. *Tonight,* he thought, *I'm looking more like Spike.*

The katydids were not the only things chirping in the warm southern air as the clock moved toward midnight. Something was buzzing inside him, something keeping him stirred up and awake — a plan perhaps, more a contemplation taking shape.

He was two months shy of his thirty-sixth birthday, separated from his wife, and sleeping in the front bedroom of the small rental house in which he had grown up. Things had not gone as he had imagined.

He had launched into the establishment of his own finance company against his wife's advice. She did not trust his partners, or maybe even his judgment, and it turned out she was right. He questioned his judgment now, regretting the day he ever started down this path. There were betrayals, and irregularities (money gone) — all on his watch. The business failed. Legal issues loomed, maybe even prison for somebody. Investors, people he knew well and had recruited throughout his hometown, were rightfully angry, and he felt responsible.

He was a popular guy, involved in the community: a Mason, a Shriner, a Jaycee, a regular at the country club. It mattered to him, maybe more than most, what people thought of him. He was not sure he could get his reputation back.

It was no wonder he could not sleep. And, of course, there was always the arthritis — rheumatoid, had it since childhood, caused him to miss a grade or two in elementary school, bedridden. It made the knees on his rail-thin legs swell, and when it flared up, it made the ever-present slight limp become more pronounced.

He quietly slipped from the front bedroom of the little mill village house his mother had rented forever, trying not to disturb her sleeping as he made his way past her bedroom toward the kitchen in back. He stepped out onto the rickety wooden porch and down the three brick steps that led to where his car was parked, careful not to let the screen door slam (as it so often did). He drove down the gravel driveway, parking lights only, and glanced one final time across the street to his right at the white-shingled house where his sister and her family lay, oblivious to the tragedy that was about to unfold.

It is somewhat ironic that this trip would take him from the village of Watts Mill to the city of Laurens, only two miles away. A stranger would not make any distinction between the two communities, would not realize he had moved from one to the other — but the residents knew the difference. He had been trying to leave Watts Mill his whole life. He harbored aspirations beyond the weaving rooms with which his parents were so familiar — well, at least his mother, who labored faithfully until she was in her seventies. His father, a musician by trade and temperament, seldom stuck with anything much, but he had been given a job at the mill to lead the band.

Nobody knows exactly the route he took, the places he gazed upon, the memories he relived, the thoughts he had. Surely, he rode around what the locals called "The Square" — the downtown area with an imposing historic courthouse at the center bounded by stores and offices that lined each of the four streets that comprised a square around it. His office had been among the businesses that lined the south side of the configuration, next to the "dime store" and down from the movie theater and the men's store where he bought his suits. Just a few years before, he had chauffeured Miss Laurens along the same route in the Christmas parade as she waved to the crowd, perched above the back seat of the convertible he drove. Those had been happier times.

Perhaps he passed by the school from which he graduated, the old Laurens High School that was converted to Central Elementary, where his only child had just completed fourth grade. It was near the savings and loan where his wife worked.

He certainly drove by the two-bedroom house on tranquil Farley Avenue where his wife and little boy were sound asleep. Perhaps he lingered there, wistful for the days when they were together, regretful for the drama that took place there on the weekend just past, or maybe his thoughts were darker. Did he consider going in?

He wound up four blocks away. There he parked his stylish, white Buick next to a grocery store that had a telephone booth beside it. The telephone booth was apparently the key. He called his baby sister Martha in Atlanta — maybe others, certainly one other. He told Martha he loved her and for her to tell her husband, Bill, to take care of her. She sensed what was coming and was frantic that she could not stop it.

He returned to the car, took a 25-caliber Beretta pistol from the glove compartment, put it to his right temple, pulled the trigger. There was a flash in the night, and everything about him — everything he had done, and everything he hoped to be remembered for — was swallowed up in that one final act. You cannot get to any of the other stuff without going through the end. It was front page in the newspaper. It is the first thing anyone thinks of when they think of him.

Arthur James Wooten Jr. — Jim to his friends, Daddy to me — became a Suicide.

And I, in ways that I am still trying to deal with, became the Suicide's Son.

Chapter 2

PAPA AND MOTHER RENEE:
THE LOINS FROM WHICH HE SPRANG

Arthur James Wooten Jr. was born on a hot August day in 1926 in the small town of Whitmire, one of several South Carolina sites to which his childhood took him as his restless father kept looking for a place to land. Arthur Sr. (Papa) was the original "rolling stone," it seems. Like the proverbial hat in the song, wherever he chose to set his things down for a spell became his home until the itch to move on hit him. (Both of my grandfathers had that quality — wandering Wootens and wandering Willards, I call them.) Glen Campbell (and others) used to sing *My Elusive Dreams,* a song about a man whose wife must surely get tired of following him across the country in pursuit of the dreams and schemes that never seem to come to fruition. Arthur Sr. could have written those lines. His wife, Irene (Mother Renee), was the stable one — and at some point, she grew tired of trying to prop him up amidst all the unsettledness. With four young children in tow, she said, "I'm going home to Laurens, and you can come if you want to." He eventually did, though he was still prone, from time to time — usually after a payday — to disappear for a while, doing God knows what.

Papa was twenty years older than Mother Renee. She was eighteen when this thirty-eight-year-old man came calling at her house. "I just thought he was coming around to see my daddy," she used to say, "but before I knew it, we were married, and he was taking me home with him." It was not a marriage made in heaven, but she stuck with him to the end of his life, some forty-three years.

Born in 1884, Papa hailed from what is called "the Dark Corner," moonshining country up in the mountains where northern Greenville County borders North Carolina. Folks "in them hollers" were clannish and peculiar, headstrong and a little (make that a lot) suspicious of outsiders. Arthur carried those qualities with him throughout his life, but he also carried a gift and a love for music — not the banjos and bass fiddles of mountain music, but the sweet sound of the saxophone. Music — and maybe wanderlust — took him out of the mountains.

Apparently, he began to play in combos and bands and his quest took him to far-off places — and his family in the Dark Corner never really knew where he was for long stretches of time. The tale was always told (I do not know if it is really true) that the twenty-eight-year-old Arthur had written to tell them that he was coming home from Europe, earning his passage by playing with a group of musicians on the maiden voyage of the Titanic. For weeks they thought he may have perished, until one day he just showed up — not thinking to let them know his plans had changed and that he was okay.

It *is* true that he joined the US Army and served during World War I. He loved to tell of how he played first chair saxophone in the Army band during those days, and the most animated I ever saw him in his old age was when he would get out albums of John Philip

Sousa marches and make me sit and listen as he "conducted" them, for my "musical education and entertainment." (I always wondered how my older cousins knew when this opportunity was coming and managed to disappear.)

Papa, by that time, was at the apex of his eccentricity. He scared me a little — intimidated me. I do not think I was the only one. I do not remember my father (or anyone else) being close to him. Papa was short (shorter than my father) and balding, with very thin wisps of white hair. (The Emperor in *Star Wars* comes to mind.) He talked with a rasp from his long years of smoking unfiltered Pall Malls, and his gnarly fingernails bore the tobacco stains that came from his habit. He mostly stayed in his room when the family was around. Yet strangely, every time I hear Dan Fogelberg's *Leader of the Band,* I think of him (and my father) with wistfulness — and every time Fogelberg sings of how his father's blood runs through the instrument he plays and of how his father's song stirs in his soul, I think of the love of music that both my grandfather and father passed down to me. My son, a chemical engineer by day, has played and sung in the same classic rock band on weekends for over twenty years, and my daughter had a music scholarship to college before opting for a degree in political science. Papa's music is in there somewhere.

Mother Renee used to say Papa's gift for music was a blessing and a curse. He would rather be making music than working, and he never really seemed to figure out how to make a living playing music on a consistent basis. In Laurens, he was, for a time, the leader of the Watts Mill band. In those days, the mills provided opportunities for entertainment and social outlets for the workers and their families, and they recruited talented people to "work" in the mill so they could excel at these extracurricular roles where they were needed. The most famous of the Wootens I know in South Carolina was a distant cousin, Earl Wooten, who paved his way through the textile baseball (and basketball) leagues to a major league position with the Washington Senators in the late 1940s.[3] His fame in South Carolina may have been even greater in basketball, and I grew up hearing of his legend. I remember the sense of amazement and family pride I felt when I learned that, in reminiscing about all the talented basketball players who played in tournaments at the iconic Textile Hall, the former manager of the facility said the best he ever saw was "either Earl Wooten or Pete Maravich ... probably Earl Wooten." I had seen Maravich. It was hard to imagine someone could have been more captivating than he. Even to this day, Earl's legend lives on around these parts.[4]

Papa's talent was musical, not athletic. He parlayed his skill into a plum position leading the band — until he wandered off to something else, too stifled by the mill routine. His children did not want to be confined by the mill either. They aimed for something more. They were all diligent students. Emily, the oldest, was trained as a nurse and married a career Army man, moving all over the world. The one time she chose to spend the months of one of her husband's battleground deployments back home in Laurens, she leased one of the biggest mansions on West Main Street. Looking back, I think it was her way of making a statement.

Mary dreamed of being a nurse as well, but because she had

contracted rheumatic fever, she was disqualified from nursing school. Instead, she stayed close to home (living across the street from her home place) and carved out a career working as a secretary for an attorney and state politician in town. Her husband, Grant, helped manage the bustling hardware store located on the Square. Martha, the baby, became a bank teller, married an engineer, and moved to the big cities of Atlanta and Greenville, but came home often to be with her mother. Despite the handicap of missing two or three years in elementary school (bedridden with rheumatoid arthritis), Jim was the first to go to college, spending two years at nearby Presbyterian College in Clinton, before venturing into business.

They all may have longed, like their father, for something more — but it was the work ethic and dignity of their mother, who operated the looms of the Watts Mill every day until she was seventy-one, that inspired them to strive to do something about it. She provided for her four children, sometimes single-handedly, on an extremely limited income. Though never wealthy, she came from a more conventional family background than Papa. Her father was Alfred Franks, a farmer, and her mother, Dora Todd (the family always said they were kin, through her family, to Mary Todd Lincoln). Miss Martha Franks, a noted Southern Baptist missionary to China, was Mother Renee's cousin, and her visits back home on furlough always presented opportunities for the family to go as a group to church and hear firsthand the reports from the mission field.

Mother Renee was a true saint, a simple woman who was faithful in every commitment she made — to her family and to her employer, and especially to her Lord. Despite hardship, she was the most positive and affirming person imaginable. She was the spiritual influence in the lives of each of her children and her grandchildren, even if none were able to live up to her example. She was never over-bearing in her religious convictions, but, by deed and consistency, she set a lofty example. Both my cousin Renee and I remember being taken to her church "circle" meetings as little kids, coloring in "color books" as she and her friends studied about, prayed for and gave money to our missionaries.

My father's Bible carries the inscription in her handwriting: "This book will keep you from sin, and sin will keep you from this book." I have wondered at what point she gave it to him — whether it was in his younger years, or after she experienced some of the trials of raising a teenage boy.

My father could be rowdy, I am told. One of his best friends from his younger days (a man in whose wedding I was the ring bearer, and who, ironically, was a deacon in a church I later served as pastor) recounted a time when my dad — this 5'7", slightly built, arthritically hampered young man — took on a Marine in a bar over some insult that was hurled. "Your daddy held his own," he said. That scene stood out to his buddy because it was both uncharacteristic in its physicality — and yet extremely telling in terms of his feistiness, his determination not to let his arthritis limit him, and his willingness to defend his honor and that of his friends. "He was the best friend anybody could ever ask for," my deacon said, years later, "loyal, fun to be around. I miss him, even after all this time."

When I heard that story, it was hard to imagine my father

in a real, honest-to-goodness fistfight. Until the last weekend
of his life, I never recalled seeing any hint of overt agitation in
him. That was not his personality. He was alternately playful and
pensive — but seldom, if ever, agitated, in my memory. The only
physical confrontation I recall from those growing up years was
an arm-wrestling match at a lakeside party with a much bigger
opponent. Daddy may have had legs weakened by arthritis, but he
had unusually strong arms for such a slender man. His opponent,
realizing he could not break the stalemate of evenly matched arms,
purposely bent his legs to strike my father in the knees. Daddy
winced, went limp and let out a muffled scream. It was a dirty
move, and I never liked that man again. The crowd concurred,
their cheers and laughter turning to jeers and scolding at the lack
of sportsmanship.

What I saw on my father's face was not anger, but sadness
at the sense of betrayal by a friend — and maybe a little embarrassment. It was his friends who were indignant as the party took
an awkward turn. In retrospect, I was the one who was angry, not
my father. I was shockingly made aware in new ways of his vulnerability, and I shared both his sadness and a touch of unmerited
humiliation. So it was good for me, as an adult, to hear of the
night my father took on the Marine and "held his own."

The truth is, whatever waywardness may have come into his
life, Mother Renee's influence of kindness and humility managed
to leave its mark on his persona. He was, at his heart, a kind and
thoughtful man, gentle of spirit. I do not remember him having
a temper or a short fuse. Whatever temper I may possess came
from the Willard side of the family.

Daddy was like his mother in his work ethic as well. Like his father, he may have been idealistic, restless for something better — but, unlike his father, he was always willing to work for it and always kept a job. He played hard and partied much — but when it came time for business, he was more than willing to put in the hours and the effort to succeed.

Sometimes a work ethic and a winning personality are not enough to overcome other factors working against you.

Chapter 3

Laurens: The Town That Shaped Him

Think of the stereotypical, small, county-seat southern town from the mid-twentieth century, and you probably have a reasonable idea of the city in which my father grew up. The eleventh largest city in South Carolina (out of forty-six counties) in the 1960 census, Laurens was maybe a *little* larger than most southern county-seat towns, but it was no metropolis. It had maintained that identity throughout his lifetime.

Then, as now, an imposing courthouse built in 1838 occupied the center of the town. A Confederate monument, erected after the Civil War, still presides over the four-acre grounds. The courthouse was bounded on four sides by streets that formed a square, with businesses and stores lining each street, facing inward toward the courthouse. Drivers accessed "the Square" at each corner, coming from the surrounding neighborhoods. The city had grown to include businesses, and public buildings and churches that worked their way outward from the city center. The savings and loan where my mother worked and the Episcopal church my father and I attended were a couple of blocks down West Main; the building that once served as his high school and then served as my elementary school was a couple blocks out West Laurens

Street. By 1960, a "bypass" opened the way for drive-in restaurants and the like, but the heart of Laurens remained, as it had his whole life, in the charming and thriving downtown.

The city and the county bear the name of Henry Laurens, a political leader in the Revolutionary War era who succeeded John Hancock as president of the Second Continental Congress. As ambassador to the Netherlands during the war, he was captured at sea by the British and imprisoned for years in the Tower of London, until returning home in a prisoner exchange for none other than Lord Cornwallis in 1781. In 1783, he accompanied Ben Franklin, John Adams, and John Jay to negotiate the peace accords in the Treaty of Paris.[5]

My father loved to tell the tale of how the city was supposed to be laid out in a different location, but Henry Laurens got drunk and confused and moved the boundaries a good half mile away. I do not doubt that, as a wealthy Charleston merchant, rice planter and slave trader, Laurens may have been known to imbibe a little too much. However, I am fairly sure he never even set foot in his namesake city, much less have anything to do with planning its parameters. Still, I loved to hear the tall tales my dad would use to entertain me. He told me about Mary Musgrove, who took food to a Revolutionary soldier hiding under the waterfall of her father's mill, with the British lurking nearby (which may be a mixture of legend and fact). He told me that Andrew Johnson, the seventeenth president of the United States, once operated a tailor shop right on the Square that comprises the city's downtown. It turns out that was definitely factual. My dad planted in me the seeds of a love of history, as well as an appreciation for a good story. He learned those things growing up in that small southern town.

Both of my parents' families had deep roots in Laurens County. Earlier generations had their share of farmers (it was the rural South, after all), but in the early 1900s the Laurens Cotton Mill and the Watts Mill, and then the Laurens Glass Plant, drew a lot of those farmers into the workforce. My parents' generation set their hearts on a different life than working in the mill. I really do not think my mother ever saw herself as "coming from the mill," though she attended school on that side of town during the years she lived there. My father, however, seemed driven to escape some perceived stigma associated with mill life. He always claimed that he did not technically live in Watts Mill, and it was true — his street (ironically, Watts Street) was barely inside the Laurens city limits. His older sisters graduated from Ford High, the mill school. He attended Ford, but whether by maneuvering or by a change in school boundaries, he and Martha graduated together in 1947 from Laurens High in town.

Daddy went to Presbyterian College (just eight miles away in Clinton, South Carolina) for two years. When he married, every house he lived in locally was in Laurens city proper, not the Watts Mill area. When he chose a place of business, he opted for a spot downtown, on the Square. I think that decision was more than a business strategy; for my father, I think it meant he had "arrived." It felt that way to me. It seemed everyone downtown knew him … and me. When I would go with him to his office, I had my routines and hangouts just like he did: drinking a Dr. Pepper at Pete Mitchell's café on the corner, reading comic books under the watchful eye and welcoming presence of "Missy" Barnes at Professional Drug Store, ordering hot Spanish peanuts at the "dime store" (Ben Franklin's Five and Dime), catching a Saturday matinee at the Capitol Theater, visiting my Uncle Grant at the hardware store and my Aunt Mary upstairs in the law office where she was a secretary. (I still remember her letting me put a nickel and two pennies into an old-fashioned Coke machine and sliding out an ice cold, six-ounce glass bottle of Coca-Cola. My soft drink addiction apparently began on those jaunts around the Square.) Whenever I hear lyrics from the James Taylor song, "Her Town Too," I think of my father and me — and of the town that shaped us both. Long ago, it used to be his town — and it used to be my town, too. When I completed my seminary education, my first pastorate back in my home state brought me back to our old town. I am still drawn to it.

One of his contemporaries, looking back to those long-ago days, opined that "Laurens was not always an easy place to break into, socially. You were either 'in' or you were 'out.' " Though she and her husband were successful professionally and financially, that observation may have reflected her own Watts Mill roots. I asked which my father was — "in" or "out"? She said, "In between." I have wondered if that was how he felt.

One of his best friends was the publisher of the local newspaper, a man I think would have made a good character in a John Grisham novel — educated, open-minded, kind of a maverick who was both a vital part of the community and yet a challenger of the status quo. I am told he took the basement floor of the newspaper office and made a "hangout," complete with a kitchen, where his cronies (many of them attorneys, businessmen and law enforcement officials) would join him for sessions of tall tales and some serious poker games. My father was in that group. One of their mutual friends told me of the time when a teenager stole the newspaper's company vehicle and hijacked it to Myrtle Beach. It was my father whom the publisher called to drive him to retrieve the car. It was just another adventure. Who knows what other stops they made along the way? One of the things that impressed me about the story was the fact that the newspaperman chose not to press charges, saying he did not want to ruin the teenager's future. I like the fact that my father was drawn to that type of friend.

Whether from a love of his heritage or a drive for acceptance and self-worth, Daddy gave himself and his energies to the community. He joined the Laurens Jaycees and jumped in with both feet. He became a member of the Masonic Lodge in Laurens and went beyond the Masons to become a Shriner. I believe it was not only an attempt to expand his social standing, but also because he was genuinely drawn to the mission of helping children facing challenges with mobility and pain. Perhaps remembering the crippling effects of rheumatoid arthritis on his own childhood, he embraced the Shriners' motto: "No man stands so tall as when he stoops to help a child." Among the few belongings he left in this world was his Hejaz Shriner's fez.

Another was a trophy from a golf tournament at Lakeside Country Club, where he became a member. Had he lived, I believe golf would have been a forever bond between us. He bought me clubs and signed me up for lessons with the club pro, Earl Tinsley.

Years later, when I returned to Laurens, I played the course with that same pro, along with a couple of my church friends. When I hit my drive off the first tee, ole Earl croaked, "Do not tell anyone I gave you lessons! You will ruin my reputation!" It was the kind of banter I remembered between them long years before. My father's golfing (and gambling) buddies were some of the leading businessmen in town, and many had a social standing that he may have envied, or at least desired. I think that may have been some of his undoing.

One of the saddest memories I hold occurred at that country club. Back then, a slot machine was a fixture somewhere in one of the back rooms. It took nickels, if I remember correctly. I loved any kind of game, and giving me a couple of rolls of coins to put into the slot machine was one of the ways Daddy could keep me occupied while he did more serious gambling in another room. Sometimes I would swim, sometimes I would play golf — but sometimes I would play the slot machine until the coins ran out and the machine would not give any more back to me. On one occasion, my ammunition spent, I went looking for him to get reloaded. I tentatively opened a door I was apparently not supposed to open, into the room where some of the men I knew from around town were seated at a table playing cards. I saw my dad. His elbow was propped on the table, with his head bent and resting in his hand, fingers through his hair. I saw a look that is hard to describe — ashen, defeated, sick. Someone else was raking in what looked like a bunch of money, and I instinctively knew he had lost big ... probably more than he should ever have bet.

Something in that scene signaled the unhealthy yearning and the reckless decision-making that lay somewhere at the base of all that went wrong in his life. I closed the door before he could see me.

Chapter 4

Colleen: The Girl He Married

When the young Carlton Willard (age nineteen) and his even younger wife, Myrtle Osborne (age sixteen) had a baby girl on December 15, 1929, in the small town of Laurens, South Carolina, they named her after two Hollywood stars: Barbara (for the striking newcomer Barbara Stanwyck) and Colleen (they pronounced it Co-leen) after another then-famous actress. I believe it was Colleen Moore, a silent picture star whose popularity rivaled Clara Bow in the '20s. In a childhood portrait, the young Colleen Willard sports the same Dutch-boy bobbed haircut that the actress made famous. The names came to fit the woman she became. When she grew to adulthood, she bore the stylishness of Moore and the independence and strength that defined Stanwyck.

Carlton, the tall, lanky, handsome son of a policeman in town, went to work firing the furnaces in the "glass plant," the main industry in Laurens. The plant produced bottles, primarily for soft drinks. It was a career that would take him to Chattanooga, Atlanta and Modesto, California — maybe some other stops along the way. Myrtle, Colleen, and her younger brother Charlie went with him to Chattanooga. Mama always spoke nostalgically of that epoch of her childhood, of riding her bike and gazing from her home on Signal Mountain across the valley to Lookout Mountain (or vice versa). It was probably there her parents' marriage broke up, because Myrtle wound up back in Laurens and Carlton eventually went to California. It was a very unsettled childhood from that point forward. Myrtle married twice more; Carlton at least three times more.

Mama went to Ford School in Watts Mill as a child. In her teenage years, she was sent back to Chattanooga to live in a Catholic girl's school, though neither parent lived there at the time. I am not sure if it was because she was "acting out," or because she and her mother did not get along amid Myrtle's unsettled life, or maybe something even more dramatic. There have been times when I have wondered if she was pregnant and went away to have a baby. I do not think so now. Pictures taken of her then show a willowy, stylish teenager at what appears to be a 1940s Tennessee mountain version of a prep school — no hint of a pregnancy or the kind of austere setting I imagine for such a situation. (I suppose I have watched too many movies.)

My best guess is that the choice to send their daughter to this private school was set in motion by something else, probably instigated by her strong-willed and more ambitious father, Carlton, within the chaos of a messy divorce. Whether this move was spurred primarily by guilt or by the desire of one spouse to exercise control over the other is hard to say. The decision could have been motivated by something as selfish as the convenience of one less encumbrance as they each tried to get a fresh start, or by something as altruistic as a genuine aspiration for a brighter future for a daughter in whom they saw possibility. I am not sure. Likely, all those impulses were at play.

I know she did not like it there — and when she got her chance, showing the blaze of self-reliance that would characterize her life, she fled. She did not go home to her mother. At the age of sixteen, she hitchhiked across the country to California to be with her father (and maybe her brother, Charlie). The woman my father married was tough, headstrong, determined — and took no guff off of anybody.

Eventually, both Colleen and Charlie wound up back in Laurens, where he attended and graduated from Ford High School. It's not clear where she graduated — Chattanooga, California, or Ford — but I know she went on to business school. I have her report cards: all A's, one B+. She secured a job at WLBG, the local radio station, and as a bookkeeper at the Buick dealership. She was smart and hardworking, never at a loss for employment, even when her journey took her to new cities. In a lot of ways, she was ahead of her time in terms of being a professional woman. In her mid-20s, she became a teller in a savings and loan office and carved out a career in which she excelled and advanced. When she died in 1975, at the still tender age of forty-five, in an era when management was still comprised of men, she trained the managers of one of (if not *the*) largest savings and loan institutions in the state. If she had lived long enough or if she had come a little later, she would have *been* the manager. Organized, personable, refined, fashionable — she came to exude professionalism and class.

Colleen was just nineteen or twenty when she and my dad started to date. I am not sure where and when my parents met, but

I know they traced their courtship to Curry's Lake, one of those small lakes that served as a hangout in many a small southern town in those post-war years — with a small beach, diving platforms and big sliding boards for swimming by day; a bowling alley, a band stand and dance floor for teens and young adults at night. Mama loved the movie *Picnic,* nominated for Best Picture in 1956. The scenes and the setting, I think, reminded her of those courting days six years earlier at Curry's Lake. I have wondered if I was conceived there, despite the watchful eye of Mr. Curry who tried to keep tabs on any shenanigans going on there.

They were young, but they were not kids. Jim was twenty-four, Colleen was twenty-one when they married on April 13, 1951. The wedding took place in the home of Dr. Ed Rouse, the pastor of the First Baptist Church (where neither attended). It was apparently a hurry-up affair. As far as I know, no one else was with them. I was born eight months later. My mother used to say I was born prematurely — but at ten pounds, I doubt that is so. Later, as an adult, after she had died, I took note of their marriage date and put two and two together. I asked my Aunt Martha about it, and she confirmed that my mother was expecting a baby when they were wed. She also told me that, because my mother had also been dating someone else, there was some speculation about whose baby I was — though she was quick to say that neither my father nor she ever doubted that I was his child. When she told me this, I thought of the term "skeletons in the closet" and questioned if I should have brought it up, but I am glad I did. This is just another example of things I wish we had talked about when my mother was alive. I understand why we did not, but I wish we had.

I also deliberated if I should write of it. Does it matter in the story? Does it make how I experienced my father's death any different? Probably not. Yet, it seemed to me to omit it would leave the picture a little less clear. And is that not a major part of the problem anyway, this tendency to hide and obscure the facts. Tyler Perry — the humorous and inspirational writer, director and actor whose own challenging family journey shaped his career and his message — places some very pertinent words in the mouth of his alter-ego Madea in one of his books: "Everybody's got skeletons in the closet. Every once in a while, you've got to open up the closet and let the skeletons breathe. Half the time, the very thing you think is gonna destroy you is the very thing nobody cares about. My advice to people is to dust them off every now and then … ."[6] So much of this account is a dusting off of the skeletons in the closet, but I am thinking that it is healthiest for me and anyone who reads this to let those skeletons breathe.

Ironically, in reconnecting with one of my mother's best friends after all these years, I discovered why the speculation existed, as well as why my father never questioned my pedigree. While she did not know what my aunt had told me, Mama's old buddy recounted my mother's courting days … of a boy named Rossie that all the girls thought was a dreamboat, and of a boy named Richards that my mother worked with at the radio station. Then she called the name of the man Aunt Martha had mentioned, a man of some prominence in town in those days, a little older than my mother. "Oh, we all used to go out to eat and go dancing," she said, referring to her husband, and to Colleen and her boyfriend. "Your mama was a good dancer and so was he. They shined on the dance floor, and just had the best time being together. She was such a happy person and had the best laugh." Then she said, as if to clarify, "But they were just friends. There was no passion between them." She hesitated, looking for words: "He had been in the war … he was wounded … he couldn't … you know … perform." All of this, unsolicited. I felt mildly amused, and a tad uncomfortable, to be listening to this ninety-something woman speaking of such things — but little did she know that she had explained a lot, solved a mystery, laid to rest a lingering question. In another conversation, I asked her if things had been different for the man my mother dated before my father, did she think they would have married. Without hesitation, she said, "Oh yes, I think so. I think they were really fond of each other." He did marry later in life. He never had children."

Despite the shaky start and the tragic finale to my parents' relationship, they had the makings of a good team, in so many ways. He was the dreamer; she was the practical one. He was playful; she was perfectionistic. They needed each other to balance themselves, if they could figure how to do it. I remember them as affectionate and supportive of one another, especially in their care for me. They had a wide circle of friends and spent lots of time at the lakeside homes of some of them. Both of them were ambitious and social, and shared similar views and values. One of my lasting memories is of them cuddled on the couch, watching the presidential election returns with hopeful anticipation the year their favorite, John F. Kennedy, defeated Nixon.

Daddy's family was close, and big and boisterous compared to Mama's — and I think she was drawn to the togetherness of it all. Like anyone who ever knew Mother Renee, Mama admired and loved her. Colleen was baptized by immersion in their family church, an act that signified both her desire to belong to Jesus and her commitment to her husband's family — a longing for stability, both spiritual and familial, I suppose. I remember her wet hair, and her excitement — almost giddiness — as she crossed the church parking lot and got in the car to head home after that Sunday evening service. I must have been four or five years old, which would make her twenty-five or twenty-six.

Mama was right there in the kitchen with Mother Renee and my aunts on the many Sundays we gathered for a big dinner. Vacations to Myrtle Beach and Pawleys Island, Cherokee and Gatlinburg were often wider family affairs. She and my Aunt Martha, close in age, became the best of friends, it seemed to me. Together, they took me on a trip to Daytona when my father could not get loose from work to join them.

I am not certain when things started going south for my parents' marriage. I cannot even pinpoint exactly when it was that my father told me he was moving out of the house. Was I in third grade or fourth? I am not sure. All I really remember is the panic I felt, the unnerving unsettledness as I watched him loading his things in the car in the garage. I cried and begged him not to go. I think he shed a tear or two, as well. I know it was hard for him, and he said all the typical things about how much he and Mama loved me and made all the promises that things were not going to change for us — promises that even a child knows instinctively are hollow.

Looking back, I recall that sometime before he left, my mother (who inherited at least a touch of the Willard temper) had come home from work in a huff one afternoon, obviously agitated about something. She began packing a suitcase and announced that she and I were going on a weekend getaway to the mountains, just the two of us. "What about Daddy?" I asked. "He's not coming. This is just us ... an adventure." Part of me was excited. I am always up for an adventure, was even back then. Yet, part of me knew something was wrong. It was out of character for her to just up and do something like that. She did not seem scared. She seemed mad, and it was clear she did not want him to know where we were. We went to Asheville, North Carolina, stayed in an impressive hotel, and she tried to make it a special time for me — but her mind was stewing. I think I remember her calling him, tense words spoken.

What was it about? Did it have something to do with his moving out? Was there an infidelity she had discovered, or something else? I did not know then. I do not know now.

But I do know that after he moved out, there would come another time when my mother scooped me up on another such escapade — but that time it would be just across town.

Chapter 5

DADDY AND ME:
MEMORIES — PRECIOUS AND OTHERWISE

Making time for reminiscing to write these pages has been a gift to me. It takes me back to the "other side" of the suicide, a place I seldom go, and then only in snippets. I often get so stuck emotionally in the trauma of the dramatic events surrounding that tragedy that I forget what the relationship was like before all of that. I found a copy of my dad's high school yearbook in the Laurens County Museum and was struck by the smiling countenance of his senior picture. I have tended to remember him with furrowed brow, more burdened. I was also touched by the way he was remembered by those who edited the yearbook: winsome and lighthearted.

My father was the man who treaded water in the deep end of the pool with his arms reaching out to beckon this preschooler to have the courage to jump from the diving board. He was the one who ran (with arthritic knees) beside me when I learned to ride a bike, though he was not fast enough to keep me from hitting a tree on my maiden voyage. He was the one who let me sit in his lap and "steer" the car as we cruised country roads. The two of us took a road trip to the 1961 Masters golf tournament together, something I think we would have done more had he lived. Gary Player (whose stature and build most resembled my father's) won that year, and though we were a part of "Arnie's Army" (pulling for Arnold Palmer), he liked Player, too. The next Masters tournament I attended was over forty years later, and Gary Player was still competing. I followed him for a while, and wished my father were there so we could talk about the year we saw "the Black Knight" win his first major championship.

Daddy would often sing as we rode. I think he took being a Sinatra look-alike to heart, and as I remember it, he was a fairly good crooner as well (but I thought he sounded like Dean Martin more than Frank Sinatra). When I found that yearbook, I discovered he was in the Glee Club and the Music Club in high school. It made sense. One of the movies he took me to see was *A Hole in the Head,* in which Sinatra portrays a widower with a twelve-year-old son. In the film, father and son sing "High Hopes." I think Daddy and I both identified with the characters, and we would sing the song together for weeks after the movie came out. His favorite hymn was "The Old Rugged Cross." It was the song I remember him singing most. I can still almost detect the faint echo of his rich baritone voice, and I never hear or sing that classic hymn without thinking of him.

The only real spanking I remember, he gave to me. It was at Mother Renee's. I am not sure what I did wrong, but Daddy took me back to the bathroom where I had seen other cousins taken for their misdeeds. I do not know if he actually said it, but the adage "This is going to hurt me more than it hurts you" was written all over his face. It was a grim duty that he fulfilled reluctantly.

He popped my bare bottom with a slap that probably hurt my pride more than my rear end, but I cried like someone had stuck a thousand pins in me. The next time I was taken there, he said, "I'm going to slap my hands together and you holler, and then go out like you are pouting." It was good psychology. It was the last time I had to be "spanked" for unruly behavior at Mother Renee's.

Those vacation trips to the mountains and the South Carolina coast burn brightly in my memory. He taught me how to tie meat on a string and catch crabs in the back channels at Pawleys Island and took me on thrill-seeking roller coaster rides at the Pavilion in Myrtle Beach. One time, at the Laurens County fair, he pressed my daredevil genes a little too far. I was maybe six or seven when he lured me to ride with him on "The Bullet," strapped into a cage that spun and plunged at ungodly speeds and from extreme heights. I screamed and cried so loudly and so vociferously that he had to wave his arm through the window of the cage and yell for the operator to stop the machine — which he did — but not before it made several more spins. The day would come when I rode "The Bullet" on my own, and when I took my kids on roller coasters all over the country. That daring love of the thrill ride is part of the legacy my father passed down to me.

When I was in the second grade, he asked permission from my teacher to take me on a business trip with him to New York City. When he had free time, we toured all around. I ate my first hot dog aboard the Staten Island Ferry, watching over the railing as we chugged past the Statue of Liberty. We zoomed to the top of the Empire State Building and gazed out over the city. I was in awe of the bright lights and rapid pace of the city — still am.

I remember two funny, and somewhat poignant, incidents from the hotel where we stayed — both occurring while he was on the phone. The first happened when we were just settling in. I was ready to "do things," but he was taking care of business. In my impatience, I went out in the hall, told the elevator operator (the hotels had elevator operators in those days) to take me to the lobby floor. I strode through the ornate lobby, through the revolving doors, and out onto the busy street. I hurriedly walked around the block, exploring on my own, circled back through the lobby and caught the elevator up to our floor. I think my father was still on the phone and had no idea I had wandered beyond the hotel. It could have been a disaster.

One other time, when he was engaged in a lengthy phone conversation, he put one hand over the receiver and mouthed the words and motioned for me to pour him a drink. I was a bit honored, felt like a "big boy," that he would give me such a task — me, fixing a drink for my dad on a business trip to the big city. I knew you poured some from the bottle of bourbon and some from the bottle of Coca-Cola; I just had never paid attention to how much from each. I figured the bourbon was supposed to be the good stuff, so I poured about three-fourths of the glass from that bottle, one-fourth from the other, and added some ice. I was proud of my concoction and watched with anticipation as I handed it to him to drink. He took more than a sip, less than a swig — but enough that his eyes watered, his face contorted, as he swallowed hard. I think it took his breath away. He laughed and said, "Son, you make a strong drink." I do not remember him ever asking me again. It was probably for the best, in a lot of ways.

Alcohol was always around, but I did not think much about it then. It was part of the scenery — at the country club, at the Hub Drive-In restaurant, at the lake, I guess at home, though I do not really remember it there as much. Thinking back, we stopped at a roadside "joint" even on the way to the Masters. I remember pestering my dad in a restaurant in Charlotte to let me taste his beer. I was probably seven or eight. Our family was there for all the festivities of the Shrine Bowl football game pitting high school all-stars from South Carolina and North Carolina against one another. We were waiting for the parade to start. He had a draft beer, and I kept saying, "Let me try it." He would slide the mug away from me. It was more a game than anything, but he finally relented. I sipped it — and hated it. Maybe because of that, I have never liked the taste of beer, even when I drank it from time to time with my high school and college buddies. My parents both smoked cigarettes, as many people did in those days, and I had a similar experience with smoking — my father giving me a cigarette at an early age, I think on purpose to turn me against it. I hacked and coughed, and it tasted awful, and I never smoked again — cannot even stand to be around cigarette smoke. In a backwards way, these early encounters with alcohol and tobacco steered me away from behaviors that caused problems for my father and others in our family.

The only time I recall being troubled by his drinking involved an incident at my grandmother's house. The family gathered in the kitchen, around a table full of food — a Sunday dinner or a holiday feast. The women were busy, scurrying around with last-minute tasks, moving hot food from the stove to the table and making sure each dish had a serving spoon or fork. In her busyness, Mother Renee did not see that my dad was holding a beer in his hand as he came into the kitchen — but I saw. It was something that she did not approve of, and it would really hurt her feelings if she had seen. I do not know if he just absentmindedly brought it in with him from outside, or if he was deliberately trying to sneak it in — but as we all assembled in a circle for the blessing, he positioned himself behind someone else. As everyone bowed their heads, he saw me looking across the room at the beer can in his hand. He grinned, put the can behind his back, and held his finger to his mouth as if to say, "Shhhh" — probably because in my precociousness at that immature age, I might have been prone to say, "Look what Daddy has in his hand." I did not say anything, but something about that scene troubled me then, and troubles me now. I thought it was disrespectful to his mother, and, somehow, I felt like he brought me into the conspiracy to disrespect her, like "We are going to fool her." I know now his behavior was juvenile and stood in contrast to the way I usually saw him — serious, responsible, reliable. It disappointed me.

In retrospect, alcohol was a more severe problem for him than I think I had ever realized, and may have ultimately been the key to his undoing. When I was in seminary and took counseling courses, I remember learning that, while Baptists (at that time) — because of their traditional emphasis on abstinence — drank a lot less than members of other denominations that promoted moderation, those Baptists who *did* drink were much more likely to become alcoholics than others. I do not remember the exact statistics, but they were somewhat startling. The theory was that the guilt from going against the teachings of their faith and the judgment it engendered intensified any issues they had with alcohol. That kitchen scene came back to me in class that day. It was not just that my father drank, but that he had to hide it from the person he looked up to the most. It went against the faith and values he was taught.

He grew up and was baptized in the Lucas Avenue Baptist Church at Watts Mill. One of the great gifts that came to me nearly four decades after his death was to connect with one of his childhood friends (a man who worked at a funeral home in Greenville where I conducted a lot of funerals as a minister). He told me about growing up with my father in Laurens, and about the night he and my father accepted Christ at a revival at Lucas Avenue and got baptized together. He spoke with such affection of my father, and of what a good person he was. They went to church together through their growing-up years. It was the same church I remember my mother being baptized in as an adult in her 20s. So there were family roots in Lucas Avenue. I remember going there to Sunday School, Training Union, and children's choirs some when we lived in Laurens — but I associate it with Mother Renee more than my parents. It seems they drifted away from Lucas Avenue. Some of it was from moving around — we lived in Anderson and Union for two years. Some of it was life choices and misplaced priorities — spending Sundays at the lake and the country club. Some of it was, I think, that they did not feel like they fit in that particular church.

In fairness, while Mother Renee may have been the strongest spiritual example and influence in our family, I must credit both my mother and father for trying to instill Christian teachings in my life. I remember them teaching me to say my prayers every night: "Now I lay me down to sleep." I remember my mother taking me to a revival service at a church down the street from our house in Union and telling my father (who had gotten home from work late) how proud and surprised she was that this squirmy six-year-old had sat still and quiet through the whole sermon. (It was of the "hellfire and brimstone" variety, roared by a very loud and animated preacher. I was afraid to breathe, much less to move.) I was always in Vacation Bible School every summer, and they worked with me on "Bible drills" to the point that I excelled in the competitions. I am not sure I have given them enough credit down through the years for some of those formative lessons.

And one other thing occurs to me when I consider these memories of life before the suicide: It was they who set a standard of respect for all people regardless of race. I grew up in the segregated South of the 1950s and early '60s. Obviously, there was a lot of racial prejudice in the community in which I grew up, as there was in pretty much every southern town back then. (Years after both of their deaths, one of the old movie theaters in Laurens was turned into The Redneck Shop, specializing in rebel flags and other Confederate memorabilia — a scourge on the reputation and thorn in the side of that town.) In talking to one of my childhood friends as I researched this book, I was reminded of examples of harsh realities about the way things were, and I remember my father in particular being troubled by it.

My parents were products of their time and culture, so I am sure they had blind spots. I am sure I do as well. However, I never heard racial epithets or prejudicial remarks in my house growing up. My mother worked, so we had African-American maids — but both of my parents treated them with graciousness and respectfulness, and taught me to do the same (except the time when, as a four-year-old, I locked Lizzie out of the house — but that is a story for the next chapter). In my recollections, both of my parents exemplified kindness and humility in their dealings with *all* people.

Toward the end of his life, my father began attending the small Episcopal church in Laurens. I imagine, amid his struggles, he was trying to find a place to worship where he did not feel the extra weight of judgment that came with his drinking. He was searching for something— and, in his search, he took me with him. Among my most cherished memories are those of kneeling beside him on the prayer rails that extended from the pews in that little sanctuary, him helping me read from the Book of Common Prayer, reciting together the Apostle's Creed. He was looking for grace that was greater than all his sin — and considering the decision he made to end his life, I guess one would be prone to say he did not find what he was looking for (at least in this life), that it was too late.

I am hopeful that he found that grace beyond this life — that if the son he left behind could forgive his fragility and try to understand his desperation, then surely would not the One he called Father, Perfect in His love, forgive him, too?

I do not know. That is just one of the questions that has jangled around in my mind and in my heart these nearly sixty years since.

Chapter 6

300 FARLEY AVENUE: THE HOUSE WE LIVED IN

In some ways, Jim and Colleen carried on the tradition of the wandering Wootens and the wandering Willards. They moved a lot, especially in those early years — both trying to find or further their career paths.

I remember, at the age of three and four, living in a small house right behind Pigg's Grocery Store, out South Harper Street on the southern edge of town. (Ironically, it was at the phone booth beside that store, in sight of the house where we once lived, that my father took his life.) It was in that home that I dialed the number for my mother's workplace to tell her that Lizzie, our maid, was gone. In truth, I had locked Lizzie out of the house when she went to hang clothes on the clothesline in back. I can still see her standing at the door, rattling the doorknob and peering in the window. I can still hear her frantic voice, "Jimmy, let me in. Let me in this house right now!" Lizzie was a good soul, as I remember — but I apparently wanted my mother at home. I had to apologize.

We moved from there to Anderson, South Carolina, where I went to a nursery school/kindergarten and refused to take naps. On the other side of our small rental duplex lived the aunt and uncle of the girl I would one day marry. Her grandmother remembered me as a five-year-old and told funny stories about me from a birthday party I attended. Small world.

We made our way from Anderson to Union, South Carolina, where I started school and got "popped with a yardstick" for talking too much and getting out of my seat to kiss a little girl on the cheek. We lived in a rental house in the mill section of town, where the coal furnace blew the warmest air through the grate in the floor of the hallway, and where I swear I heard reindeer scratching on the roof the one Christmas we lived there.

In each of those towns (and even a brief stint in Spartanburg in my infancy), my father worked for a finance company and my mother took a job either in bookkeeping or secretarial work. They were young and trying to find their way, but the way led back home.

We returned to Laurens in time for the second grade, residing at first in a rental house on Moreland Avenue before buying a house a block or two away. I suspect my mother was the driving force in settling down, getting equity instead of "throwing away" money on rent. For someone whose family life was marked by unsettledness, security (especially financial security) reigned supreme in her mindset. She had found her calling, carving out a career in the savings and loan business that lasted the rest of her too-brief life. It was a perfect fit for someone as practical, professional and numbers-oriented as she — and I am sure that dealing with loans and mortgages every day sensitized her to the need to make a sound investment herself.

Of course, the white house on the corner of Farley Avenue and Chestnut Street appealed to Jim, too. It was in an established and respected neighborhood in the "city." It sat catty-cornered from Dr.

Nichols' house and down the street from Dr. Dusenberry's house, on a broad avenue lined with nice homes and finely manicured lawns. The Lutheran Church was a couple of blocks down, and a little further was the local hospital. It was not West Main Street, but it was not Watts Mill. The young couple was excited about their new abode and felt like they were on their way to bigger and better things.

The house itself was relatively small, but it was neat and well-kept. Situated on a large corner lot, it boasted a tidy and appealing front lawn and a sprawling backyard, with small trees and muscadine vines marking its back boundary. Each room would play a part in the events of that tragic Father's Day weekend.

The front door opened to a relatively large living room, with a slightly elevated (two-step) dining area to the right. A wrought iron rail defined the dining room. The back wall of the living room was punctuated by two French doors that swung open to reveal a large screened-in area (the middle porch) that functioned almost like a den in warmer weather. In colder weather, it was a dangerous place for a pet parakeet to be left overnight, as the creatively named Blue Boy learned, much to his demise. That was the most haunting recollection I associated with the middle porch before my father's death.

The back wall of the living room extended all the way through the elevated dining room and was interrupted there by a swinging door that led to the small, but bright and airy, kitchen and breakfast nook on the other side. Down the steps from the kitchen was another small, screened area (the back porch) that led either straight to the garage or out the right to the side yard facing Chestnut Street. Two bedrooms and two bathrooms lined the left side of the house and were accessed through a hallway that came off the living room. My room was in the back of the house; my parents' room was in the front.

When I recall my childhood, it is that house I think of — playing "capture the flag" outside with the neighborhood kids, making "haunted houses" in the unfinished basement, doing homework and working on Cub Scout projects in the breakfast nook. It is where I remember happy times with my parents — getting up late at night and squeezing between them on the couch as they watched the election returns from Kennedy and Nixon; churning ice cream on the back porch on a warm summer night; sitting on the middle porch and listening to them talk about their lives. I remember when two cars collided at the intersection of Farley and Chestnut — one crashing through the wall of our dining room, and another winding up in the hedges of a neighbor's yard. My father sprang into action, going from car to car, calming and tending the injured as my mother phoned for help. I remember thinking he was a hero for how he handled such an unexpected crisis, and I was proud to be his son.

It is easy to forget — considering the drama, the turmoil and the heartache which fell upon that place — that we lived (for a time) a contented and somewhat normal family life there. It is easy to forget the sunshine that preceded the tempest, when the tempest's devastation is so brutal and life-altering that it leaves its imprint upon you forever. I do not know when the clouds first started rolling in, but I will never forget the weekend the storm burst, and nothing was ever the same again.

Chapter 7

A Bridge Too Far: The Business That Failed

It is unlikely that, while attending Presbyterian College in nearby Clinton, my father envisioned a career working for a finance company — but that is what he found. Maybe if he had gotten his degree, it would have been different — but whether from his own financial need or the responsibility of a wife and a child, he had to find a job. The job that was available was managing a finance company. At least it was white-collar, business-oriented — not like the gas station he had worked at before as a teenager, or the mill where his mother labored.

He had ability. He was recruited as a manager from one finance company after another, broadening his responsibilities and securing the modest salary increases that went with each move. Still, the business was transient. Each step usually meant a move to another town. And, in the end, the only ones making any real money were the investors who owned the companies, not the managers and employees who operated them.

Still, that was not the real problem. Offering high-interest loans to people who had money troubles and poor odds of being able to make the payments was ill-suited for his personality. For everybody you helped through a crisis, there were more whose crises only intensified with missed payments and deepening debt. He was always having to chase people down, always having to listen to excuses and often having to rework impossible situations that were only going to get worse until some action was required. I surmise all this now, seeing as an adult how such businesses work. He was too sensitive a soul to deal with that very well. He told me, on more than one occasion, "Jimmy, don't ever go into the finance business," as if an eight-year-old kid would even understand what such a career would be, much less seek such a role. I did understand that he was unhappy and wanted something different. I believe he felt stuck in that profession, and the only way to change his circumstance was to start his own business.

I picked up bits and pieces of his plan. I recall a few times riding in the car with him in the evening hours, after he got off work at the office, as he made his way through various neighborhoods in Laurens. It could be that he was merely collecting delinquent loan payments, but my sense is that he was visiting potential investors. I am guessing the deals had already been made and he was picking up checks or paperwork, because he would not be gone long as I sat in the car and waited for him to come out of the houses to which he went. I recall accompanying him all over the state (Columbia and Charleston in the daytime, must have been summertime) on what must have been organizational efforts to transfer the ownership of the business to him. Looking back, I think the trip to New York must have been related to that venture in some way. I remember going to the home of one of his "partners," a guy a little older than my dad. He lived in Greenville, was brash and overbearing, and he gave me the creeps. I liked one of the other partners okay, a younger guy who I think we had known before. I have no idea who recruited whom, whose idea it was — but although my father was to be the president of the corporation, it seemed like the big-talking guy from Greenville was the dominant force.

I guess it was because I was an only child, but I sure seemed to be around a lot when my parents had serious discussions. One of them concerned the business. They sat on the small porch or patio that was at the front of our house. It was in the cool of the evening. The gist of the conversation was that my mother, ever practical and cautious in matters of money, expressed hesitation. My father, ever the dreamer, seemed hurt by her hesitation. "You do not believe in me," he said, at one point. "Jim, I do believe in you," she said. "But I don't feel confident in some of the people you are dealing with. And I think you are bearing too much risk." They were not together on this business enterprise, at least at that point — even though several of the investors were likely people he knew through Mama's work.

I do not know how they resolved their difference of opinion, or if they ever did. I also wonder if this disagreement was the tipping point in the relationship starting to unravel. I just know he moved ahead with the project. American Credit, the business downtown on the Square, belonged to him. He was on his way. Things looked good for a while. It was a busy place, and he seemed much happier. But in the end, my mother was right.

My father's reach exceeded his grasp. The business failed, primarily because someone did something crooked. Funds were allegedly misappropriated. Investors were ostensibly defrauded.

Most of those investors were local — people who would have been known by, and perhaps friends with, my father, but not by the big-talking guy from Greenville. The word among the Wooten clan was that my father had been duped, used for his connections in the community by a crafty and crooked manipulator. Ironically, their defense of my father's character essentially assaulted his judgment. Either way, it was a devastating blow to his reputation and his sense of self-worth. In his mind, in the eyes of the town he wanted so much to value him, he was either a crook or a patsy.

Of course, as a child I did not know much about all of this. It would only be natural that as I learned of it, I would tend to accept my family's version. Yet, I remember Mother Renee and Aunt Mary speculating at the time that he really did not commit suicide, that his business partners had him killed. The only other reference I have found that promoted that theory was a letter from the attorney who argued with the life insurance company's quick denial of payment on his policy, citing suicide. The attorney pointed out that Jim had been the "only living witness in a serious fraud investigation," raising the possibility that he had been killed to stop his testimony. No other officials mentioned that likelihood, and there is no record that the attorney pursued it any further.

If some in his family could not face the truth in his death, perhaps they could not face the truth in his life. Did he defraud his investors? I do not know. My mother, who bore the financial brunt of his actions and had every reason to resent him for it, did not believe that he did. She believed his fault was found in associating himself with his partners, not in devising a scheme. She secured the legal services of her boss, a respected attorney who served as the chairman of the board of the Savings and Loan Association, to defend him when a state investigation led to charges against the officers of the corporation.

The newspaper account of the case seemed to support my mother's conclusion, as it reported that the charges against my father were dropped in exchange for his testimony. The younger associate was released on bond awaiting trial; the older remained in jail because he had other charges pending for similar misdeeds in Augusta, Georgia. I assume my father testified. I believe I recall hearing of trips to the South Carolina state capital (Columbia) to do so. Ironically, in researching the coverage of my father's death, which appeared on the front page of the June 20, 1962, edition of the *Laurens Advertiser,* I discovered a separate article reporting the indictment of his associates. I know they were both found guilty and served prison terms, but in all my research I have been unable to find the details of their trials or their sentences.[7]

Another detail stood out to me in reading those articles. The account of my father's death — which included details of when, where and how — read more like an obituary. It made no mention of the court case, but gave a brief biographical sketch, listed survivors, as well as plans for the funeral service. What caught my eye was the list of the pallbearers and honorary pallbearers. It read like a Who's Who of some of the most prominent men in the city — doctors and lawyers, elected officials, and leading businessmen. I suspect some of them may have been investors in his abortive enterprise — but the presence of so many respected citizens on that list seemed to me to be a testimony of their affirmation of, and ultimate belief in, his character, despite his failure.

I wish he could have known the support he had among these people whose judgment would have mattered so much. Shame obviously contributed to the decision to end his life, as well as guilt for the losses people he knew had suffered on his watch. I cannot fathom the pressure he must have been under, facing financial ruin, feeling betrayed by people he thought were his friends and having to testify against them. I can understand how such a burden could lead to thoughts of suicide, but according to one of his closest confidantes, it was something else that pushed him over the edge.

Chapter 8

COMING APART: THE PLOT THICKENS

Jim and Colleen, my parents, had been separated for at least a few months — maybe a year or more — when that ill-fated weekend occurred. This is the place that the sequence of events is a little muddled in my mind. I know that the business had closed and that my father had taken a job as a manager of Field Credit in Gastonia, North Carolina, in mid-September of 1961 as I began my fourth-grade year. My impression is that the separation had occurred prior to that, though I never remember him having another residence in Laurens other than staying with Mother Renee.

I went to Gastonia at least once. It must have been during a school break. My mother took me to the train station in Greenville, arranged for me to ride in a Pullman sleeper car, talked to the porter about watching after me, and told me not to leave that car until the porter told me we had arrived in Gastonia. The train collided with a car at an intersection in a town somewhere between Greenville and Gastonia. The big wheels did not keep on turning, and my curiosity got the better of me. I left the Pullman car and climbed down the steps to see if I could catch a glimpse of the wreckage. The Pullman car was at the back of the train and the collision was too far in front to see, so I climbed back up and went to my cabin and read comic books until we were moving again.

I told my dad about all the excitement, and of my attempts at trying to see the wreckage. He had been worried about the delay, so at first he mildly scolded me for leaving the train, but then he kind of laughed. I think he maybe saw a little of his own independent streak in me and took pride in it.

At night, I slept on a cot he set up for me in the room he rented through the week. In the daytime, I hung around his office and liked meeting his co-workers. I remember one was named Bunky, a younger associate, a happy jokester who made me feel welcomed. My dad and I ate at a nice restaurant in the evenings, and I think we went bowling one night. Friday afternoon came, and we drove back to Laurens. I recall that he was tired and was having a tough time staying awake. At one point, he nodded off and was terrified when he felt himself veering off the pavement just as I called out, "Daddy!" Rattled, he fussed at me for not saying something sooner. Funny, the things that come back to you.

He transferred to the Greenville office of Field Credit in April of 1962, I suppose to get closer to Laurens and cut his commute. It is amazing to me that he could continue to get these managerial positions, considering the very public legal issues he was facing. I must conjecture that those hiring him believed that the fault for the misdeeds lay somewhere other than with him. It is also amazing to me to consider how much time I spent with him in his workaday world, how much I think he really wanted to have me with him as often as he could, even if it was during business hours. I remember spending time with him at the Greenville office, too.

Years later, when I served as pastor of a downtown church in that city, some friends invited my wife and me to eat at Charlie's Steak House, which became a favorite. (The food was excellent, and the ambience made me think of the Italian restaurant in *The Godfather*, in which Michael Corleone avenges the attempted assassination of his father.) As I sat in that restaurant, it felt strangely familiar. I told my wife, "I've been here before." I glanced out the window, and across the street was a window in a store-front that I realized had once been the finance company where my father worked. I cannot describe the confluence of emotions I felt — stunned, but oddly comforted; homesick, but deeply grateful. We had eaten here together, my father and I … in this very place. So much had changed, but Charlie's still looked and felt the way it did in the early '60s, and it never failed to transport me back to that time.

Somewhere during this time of marital separation for my parents — maybe before — somebody let a stranger in. I am told now, that on the Wooten side of the family, there was the belief that my mother had a boyfriend. It may be true, but I lived with her and I never saw signs of it, though after my father's death, among her possible pursuers was the purported scoundrel — a married man of some prominence in our small southern town. The parties at Lake Greenwood were often at his place. But I only saw him come to our home once. It was in the daytime, with me there, on what appeared to me to be official business — and I know that while he may have had some interest in her, she was not too fond of him.

After most of these pages were written and I almost

miraculously found my parents' long-lost friends from years before, I asked them about the speculation on the Wooten side of the family. They both said they just did not see how that could be true, and they thought they would know.

What the Wootens supposedly did not know, and I (and apparently a lot of others) did, was that my father had a girlfriend — though I did not know who she was for nearly sixty years until these old friends told me. I knew where she lived, or at least where they rendezvoused — because I became part of a stakeout with my mother, one night not long before that weekend.

At the time, it seemed like another daring caper, much like our quick getaway to Asheville. The phone rang. Colleen answered it and quickly burst into action, hurrying me into her car. With great stealth, like detectives I saw on TV, with headlights turned off, we backed the automobile onto an empty lot across from the public library where I checked out Hardy Boys books. I felt a little like a Hardy boy myself, trying to solve some mystery.

Colleen positioned the vehicle to face the ground-level door at the back of a once-imposing, three-story white frame house — a door that led to what I now suppose was an apartment. I noticed a car that looked like my father's long, white Buick. The mystery was becoming clearer.

After maybe fifteen or twenty minutes (an eternity to a ten-year-old trying to sit quietly), there was movement. Colleen waited … one second, two seconds … then our headlights flashed on (I am sure they were on high beam). Picture those spotlights that lock in on prisoners trying to make a break from the penitentiary. The woman hid behind the man. I did not see her clearly.

The man shielded his eyes from the light, but I knew too well who he was.

The deed was done. The mission complete. Suspicions confirmed. My mother drove away without a word. I do not recall it ever being talked about again. I am sure it was, but I do not remember asking questions, and I was never there when they spoke together of it. But I remember.

Whether this episode was the breaking point — or maybe the strain of all his legal entanglements or his further struggles with alcohol or the bleakness of his future — the "other woman" apparently called it quits not too long after. According to the testimony of one of Daddy's closest friends in a conversation with my wife years later, it was the end of that relationship with the woman caught in the headlights that became the last straw in my father's struggle to hold onto his sanity or to any hope for the days ahead.

The adventure had not turned out so well for me (or for either of them, for that matter). I felt a little sick at our discovery, a little torn — sad for my mother, disappointed in my father, and strangely somehow a little guilty to have been a party to his embarrassment.

That confusing conglomeration of emotions characterize much of my psyche, whenever I think of my father.

Chapter 9

A GLIMPSE OF MADNESS: THE WEEKEND (PART I)

A whirlwind of drama descended on the little house on the corner of Farley Avenue and Chestnut Street on Father's Day weekend of 1962. I was just a kid, and it was a long time ago — and the chronology may not be exact, but the scenes are burned in my memory with vivid detail. Obviously, as a ten-year-old, I did not understand all that was going on — but I knew some things that even those adults on the periphery did not. I was there. I heard it. I saw it.

The wheels were already in motion before the portentous weekend got underway. The business venture had failed (the business venture against which my mother had advised). Legal and financial consequences loomed. The marriage had fallen apart, and so too had the relationship with the girlfriend. My father's life was unraveling. The usually nattily dressed, well-groomed young businessman who cared maybe a little too much about appearances began showing up at the Hub (his favorite hangout) unkempt, borderline disheveled. Normally sociable and good-natured, he was withdrawn and sullen. If he bothered to order food, he just picked at it. Mostly, he nursed a beer ... and then another. His drinking got worse. One of his closest friends was the owner (along with her husband) of the Hub, and he confided some of his angst to her. She listened, counseled as best she could, tried to comfort, never realizing just how dark his thoughts were becoming or the depths to which his desperation would lead him. (It was she who, those many years later at a bridal shower for her grand-daughter, told my wife, Becky, that he was especially distraught over the unnamed girlfriend's decision to end their affair.)

Strangely, his desperation led him to my mother. I still find it so odd that he would turn to her when his world was crumbling, considering the circumstances of their relationship at that moment in time. I am not sure whether it was Friday night or Saturday night (I think Saturday), but he phoned and asked if he could come over. I saw firsthand the change in his appearance — gaunt, scruffy — and his behavior was noticeably erratic, even to a child. We all sat on the middle porch. The encounter was at once both familiar and awkward — familiar, because it was the three of us together, in our house, as we once had been; and awkward, because of the gulf the weeks or months of separation had created. Tension lingered between them from words spoken and actions taken that left feelings hurt and trust broken, the tatters of a marriage that had come unglued. For a moment though, I think hope crept into that room. I know it did for me, and I think it did for them, too.

Daddy sat in a chair in one corner, Mama on the chaise lounge in another, and I (when I sat still) on a chair across the room from them. While I do not remember exactly all that was said, the conversation was civil — more than civil — warm, caring, maybe a little confessional yet guarded on my father's part, maybe a little sympathetic but guarded on my mother's part. At times he rambled a little; at times he did not complete his thoughts — perhaps alcohol was involved, but my impression is that with so many issues and emotions rummaging through his brain, he was not sure what to say or how to say it. What I clearly remember is, later in the conversation, my father talking about how he needed a haircut and had not had a chance to get one, and then asking Mama to trim his hair. A perplexed expression came upon her face, and she said, "Jim, I've never cut your hair. I have never cut anybody's hair. I'm not sure I know how." He persisted, "Just a trim — shape it up a little."

Tentatively, she went to another room to retrieve a pair of scissors and a comb. When she returned, he sat at the foot of her chaise lounge as she propped herself behind him and timidly began to snip at the edges of his locks around the ears and in the back. He continued to talk as she carefully, and with great hesitation, tried to neaten the uneven strands. At one point, she said, "Jim, I don't know what I'm doing. I'm afraid I'm going to mess up." With sudden agitation, he grabbed the scissors from her hand and snapped, "Here, just do this," as he began to indiscriminately whack away at the hair atop his head.

The eruption was abrupt, loud, unexpected, and alarming. My mother was startled, and maybe scared. She hollered, "Jim!" and reached as if to stop him — but it was over as quickly as it began. I was disturbed, and still am, by the bizarre and inexplicable display. In retrospect, it was the clearest expression of the irrationality that was eating away at him and the emotional instability that would lead to his demise. A stunned and uncomfortable silence followed his outburst, as I remember it. I do not think I cried, but I wanted to. My sense is that he left quietly shortly afterwards — embarrassed, I am sure, likely as shaken as we were, but still agitated.

The next time I saw him, he tore open the locked screen door of the porch on which we sat that night.

Chapter 10

SHOWDOWN: THE WEEKEND (PART II)

The phone rang early Sunday morning. Apparently, my father was on the other end. My mother went into a panic. Whether it was because of his volatile and unsettling flare-up when last we saw him, or whether it was because of something he said on the phone that morning, or maybe there had been some conflicting interaction between them unbeknownst to me in between those times — but my father was coming to our house, and my mother was beside herself. She told me to stay in the bedroom, but I did not. I followed her as she began going frantically through the house, locking doors. She paced in the kitchen, nervously pausing to glance out the window until finally she saw his car drive up. Others from his family were in the car with him.

We moved out of sight into the dining room, standing silently on the other side of the swinging door. Why? I had no idea. We heard the rattling of the back door, my dad calling firmly, "Colleen, come open this door." She waited. The rattling stopped. After some time, she told me to go back to the bedroom, as she prepared to go into the kitchen, presumably to see if they were gone or maybe to confront whatever was awaiting her. As I scuttled across the hardwood floor of the living room, I glanced to my right through the opened French doors to the middle porch and saw my father standing on the landing outside the locked screen door. I froze. He tugged at the door, but the latch held. He said, "Jimmy, come open the door." I could not move. I was conflicted, unsure what to do. I detected what I took to be disappointment flash in his eyes. His jaws clenched. He pulled harder at the door, and then yanked it, ripping the hook from its moorings, the force nearly tearing the door from its hinges. I ran to their bedroom and jumped in the bed, pulling the covers tight around my neck. He followed right behind, and in the commotion my mother was not far behind him.

He came only halfway into the room, apparently to keep from frightening me further. He spoke with a purposeful calmness of tone, a calmness that stood in stark contrast to my mother's obvious apprehension and the uncharacteristically strange display I had just witnessed as he entered the house: "Jimmy, I called to tell your mother that I was coming to get you to take you to the country club with me. Wouldn't you like to go play golf?" The truth was, I would love to go play golf with him. It was a bond we shared. He had paid for lessons for me, let me drive his cart when he played with his cronies (at least on courses where there were no caddies), took me with him to the Masters. But I looked over his shoulder to my mother standing in the doorway. Her eyes were wide with what looked like fear and pleading, and she was shaking her head "no," and so I said, "I don't feel like going today."

He did not argue or try to convince. He did not get mad, but I saw the letdown in his eyes ... not so much a feeling of betrayal as a sense of resignation that a battle was lost. He let me off the hook, did not try to guilt me or make me feel bad. "We'll try it another time," he said.

Of course, we never did. I often wonder what would have happened if I had chosen to go with him that day. Was that the act of affirmation that would have lifted his spirits amid the rejection and dejection he was experiencing at every turn? Did he perceive my refusal to go as just another rebuff? Such is the guilt and the self-questioning that stays with you long after a loved one commits suicide.

In that moment, I took my cue from my mother, from the look of alarm in her eyes as she tacitly pleaded for me not to go with him. The question I have now is "What was she afraid of?" Did she sense the depth of his instability (an instability I had just witnessed earlier in the weekend)? Did she fear for my safety? Or was the fear more about loss of control, with me as the pivotal pawn in the tug-of-war between them? She was a fighter and a survivor — strong-willed. Were her old familial insecurities inflamed — her father dead by suicide only a year, her relationship with her mother "complicated"? He had the bigger and closer family. Mostly, she only had me. For years, I thought the apprehension was for my safety. In recent days, I have wondered if it was more personal.

They told me to stay in the bedroom and they went to the kitchen. I snuck into the dining room and stood where my mother and I had stood earlier, listening through the swinging door, trying to figure out what was happening. I know there were other people in the room, some combination of aunts and/or uncles who came with my father. There were loud voices — arguing, accusing, and, at some point, my mother shouted, "Get out of my house." I heard scuffling sounds, something crashing and more words, and the entourage left. I later learned (1 think from my mother) that the noises I heard were from her taking a butcher knife and waving it when she told them to leave — and my father grabbing her wrist and slamming the knife to the countertop, knocking it loose.

I am not sure what it was about my mother and that butcher knife. When her friend recently recounted standing in that same kitchen listening to my mother stew about her discovery of my father's infidelity, she said my mother was washing dishes in the sink and picked up the butcher knife and spewed, "I'd like to just get ahold of her with this!" I said, "She was just talking, right?" The frail, sweet, gentle, ninety-something-year-old lady sitting before me squinted as in deep recollection and finally drawled out, "Well ... I don't know!" I guess it was that Willard temper she was remembering. (For the record, I never saw or heard tell of my mother being violent in any way or really ever much raising her voice — except the one time she slapped me for coming home inebriated and sassing her. She was just feisty.)

I have always had the sentiment that my mother was ganged up upon and that it was unfair for all those people to be there — but I suspect now that the family was there to serve not only as witnesses and support for my father, but also (even if subconsciously) to provide a safeguard against any escalation of conflict within the tensions that were running high. At least, I would like to think so.

If you had been there that morning, you would think there would never be a civil conversation between them again. You would be wrong.

Chapter 11

If I Had Known It Was Goodbye:
The Weekend (Part III)

Sometime later that day, when tempers had cooled and after a lot of soul-searching, my mother called my father and told him I had a Father's Day card I had made for him. She invited him to come to the house so I could give it to him. Whether because she felt sorry for me or sorry for him, or guilty for whatever she may have done to contribute to the trauma of the day, or whether she was hopeful for some sort of reconciliation, I do not know — but she called him, and he came.

He did not immediately enter the house. Rather, he and I walked in the backyard. I climbed up in a tree, where I was about eye-level with him. I gave him my card. I had written a Father's Day poem on the card. I also enclosed another notebook page of assorted poems that I had composed on various topics. He read them all and complimented my artistry, as only a parent can for someone with such limited poetic ability. We talked for a while and made our way onto the back porch, the smaller one between the garage and the kitchen. He sat on a small chair while I opted for the steps that led up into the kitchen. It was a nice summer afternoon — the sun in the clear, blue sky beginning its journey toward sunset, a pleasant breeze wafting through the air. Mama joined us and took a seat opposite him.

The acrimony was gone. I could tell they both regretted the events of the day and wanted to find a way forward. They spoke cautiously at first, respectfully — and, at some point, the conversation turned to their relationship. My mother told him that she loved him and wanted to work things out. He said, "I care for you and respect you so much as a mother, but I don't feel the way I should feel for us to be married anymore. I don't think there is any going back." Tears came down her cheeks; tears filled his eyes. I do not know why they chose not to ask me to go watch TV or read in my room — but I am eternally glad I heard that exchange, though it was sad for me to know that the separation was permanent. In a strange way, I found comfort in days to come from the knowledge that whatever came between them, their last moments together were tender and that they each expressed care and love for one another. When others sought to blame my mother for my father's death, I knew firsthand that she reached out to him with love and affirmation. I also knew that, though he could not reciprocate her desire to make the marriage work, his last words to her were words of praise and affirmation for her fierce devotion to and provision for his only child.

He asked if I could go with him to Mother Renee's, and she assented. I visited with family and used the waning daylight to play with cousins. As darkness approached, my father said he had a headache and went to lie down. It was the last time I saw him. I am not sure how I got home that night — my mother or a relative — but if I had known it was goodbye, I would not have left. At the least, I would have gone to him, hugged him, told him I loved him one more time.

Of course, I did not know. None of us did.

I am so grateful that, despite not knowing, I still had the chance to show him in my small way that he was important to me. I am so thankful that my mother asked him to come back over that very day, that she did not delay, and that I was able to express in writing my love for him. I still have the card and the poems I gave him. They were among the few items still in his possession that were kept and passed on to me.

I take some comfort that the last words he received from me were words of affirmation and love, written in the cursive handwriting of a fourth grader.

Happy Father's Day

Dear Daddy,
  I love you more than words can say,
  I love you in every kind of way.
  I enjoy being with you,
  Even when I'm sad and blue.

                    Love,
                    Jimmy

When I wrote those words, I did not know it was goodbye, nor just how sad and blue I was about to be.

I have often wondered if he knew that night, as he lay down, that it was goodbye.

Chapter 12

A Truth Untold: The Last Day of Innocence

I awakened on Monday morning to the unusual sight of my grandmother (my mother's mother) sitting by my bedside, apparently waiting for me to open my eyes. That had never happened before, and even in my innocence I sensed that something was wrong. Granny explained to me that my father had experienced an attack of arthritis in the night and my mother had gone to watch after him in the hospital. She and my step-grandfather John were going to take me out to their farm until my mother got back.

Her explanation satisfied me. Daddy's arthritis could be debilitating at times, though I had never known him to be hospitalized with it. My greater concern at that moment was making sure I could take my bicycle to ride and toy soldiers to play with. I spent the morning — and into the early afternoon — lost in play, riding my bike along the roads and rutted paths of their small farm. I imagine I asked if they had heard anything or if they knew when my mom was coming or when I could go to the hospital, but I do not think I was particularly alarmed.

It did seem a little odd later when they took me to Granny's brother's house, closer to town, near Watts Mill. Both Granny and John worked second shift at Whitten Village, a residential care facility for the intellectually disabled and those with special needs in nearby Clinton. They were expected to report for duty at 3:00 p.m. Uncle Bub was a mechanic and had a garage beside his house, so he was always around. He was into stock cars and used to take me for rides around the local track after the races were over. My Aunt Jeannette had taken care of me as a toddler, and I loved her dearly. Her warmth and kindness made a lasting impression, but it had been a long time since I had stayed at her house. It was a good place to go, but it did seem like it was taking a long time for my mother to come home, longer than I expected.

Cannon's Putt-Putt course was just a couple of blocks away, close enough to ride my bike. It was a simpler time, a small town where everybody knew each other, and it was no distance from the house — so nobody thought anything about letting me go by myself. I am sure they were glad to have something to keep me occupied. Cannon's had "carpet golf," in-ground trampolines, and an arcade with pinball machines. It was paradise to me — and, in retrospect, my afternoon there may have been the last truly carefree moment of my childhood and adolescence.

After an hour and a half or so, I hopped on my bike and peddled away, hoping my mother was there to pick me up. As I neared the house, I noticed two shiny black automobiles in the driveway, but I did not see our car. I bounded up the steps and into the living room and saw my mother to my left at the far end of the room, sitting on a dining room chair, with men in suits — men I had never seen — standing near her. One had his hand on her shoulder, as if to comfort her or give her support.

It was clear she had been crying, and the expression on her

face is hard to describe — weariness and sadness and anxiety and dread. It is the strangest thing — instead of running toward her, I froze in my tracks. The room was filled with silence — and apprehension. I could feel it. I asked, "What happened to Daddy?" Nobody said anything. Mama tried to speak but could not get the words out. Aunt Jeannette, seated on the couch beside the doorway where I stood, took me in her arms, hugged me as tightly as she could and then released me enough to look at me through tear-soaked eyes. She said, "Jimmy, baby, your daddy has gone to heaven."

I turned and looked at my mother. Her hand came to her mouth, as if to catch her breath before it left her or to stifle the scream that lurked somewhere deep inside. Her eyes told me what her voice could not. I ran to her, weeping, and she held me as she wept, too.

I do not remember anything else that was said. I have no idea how we got home or how my bike made it back. I suppose the men in the suits, the funeral home people or whoever else was with them, took us home. I cannot recall if anyone came to our house that night, or what we did when we got there.

I just know that something changed in me that day. The cloud came into my life. Sunshine had characterized my existence to that point. My basic personality was expectant and happy, optimistic, and adventurous. Those qualities are still with me, but from that day forward, they have been tinged with melancholy — and even when life is going just dandy, I still look over my shoulder, wondering if something bad may be creeping up on me unawares.

I woke up on June 18, 1962, ready to grab life by the tail. I went to bed knowing I would never see my father again, thinking his arthritis had taken him away.

The next day, it would get worse.

Chapter 13

SPILLED BEANS: THE STIGMA BEGINS

Death brings details to be dealt with — choose a casket or opt for cremation, decide on a venue (mortuary chapel, church sanctuary or graveside), schedule a service, meet with a minister, recruit pallbearers, negotiate financial arrangements, secure a cemetery plot, consider options for the vault in which the casket is placed. A death like my father's complicates the process. His body was thirty-five miles away, awaiting an autopsy in the morgue of the Greenville General Hospital. He was alive when the policemen on patrol found him, so he had been rushed by ambulance from the local hospital to the trauma center in the big city that was more equipped to manage such cases. He lived through the night and into the next afternoon, but despite valiant efforts, the doctors could not save him.

I have no idea when my mother took time to handle all these details, or who went with her. I am supposing it was her only sibling, her younger brother Charlie, who caught a flight from his home in Reno, Nevada, and came as soon as he heard the news — but I am not sure how quickly he arrived or at what point arrangements were made, considering the circumstances. As a minister in my adult life and from my own firsthand experiences of having to walk through such somber tasks in the loss of other loved ones, I know how gut-wrenching it can be. Thankfully, I was deemed too young to be involved in the decision-making for my father's funeral — or so one would think. Before the day was over, I would be dragged into the middle of the family frictions and assigned the role of arbiter in the last unresolved issue before preparing the obituary for publication: where the family would receive friends.

The discussion occurred at Mother Renee's house. Everything I remember about that day happened there.

The little house was crowded with people. It was hard to move from room to room without bumping into someone. People were sitting on the screened-in front porch, and on the ledges that bounded each of the three sections of the steep brick steps that led down to the front yard. Some stood by the cars in back, while the kids played nearby. Others were scattered in the living room, the small den, and the kitchen that lined the right side of the house.

At some point, I made my way inside and came into the living room. Some older folks were sitting on the couch — Mother Renee's sisters or church friends, just old people to me. My mother and others were standing in some sort of conversation. I guess they had been discussing, maybe debating, which house to list in the obituary as the place to receive friends, because as I entered the room, my Aunt Mary guided me into the group. She said, "We were just talking about what we should put in the paper about where people should come to see the family. Your mother thinks your house is easier to get to and has a little more space, but you know your daddy was not living there and we think maybe everybody should come here. I think maybe you should decide."

I felt "put on the spot." I was oblivious about where people should come. It looked to me like a lot of people had already come there without anything in the paper. I probably would have preferred for them to come to my house. I remembered when people came there for my grandfather's funeral the year before. It was home. Yet, the truth is, none of that was on my radar screen.

It obviously was a big deal to them, especially Mary. I just came into the house to get something to drink and to see what was happening. I did not want to have to settle a debate. I did not want to disappoint anyone, and I could feel the tension between them. I remember looking up from face to face at all these adults standing around me, and just kind of panicking. My mother saw the look on my face and said, "Let's just say for people to come here, and anyone who wants to come to our house will find their way."

I think now of how hard it must have been for my mother to even be at Mother Renee's, especially during such emotional turmoil. Though she had stopped by briefly from time to time to drop me off for a visit, it had been a while since she had been there with the whole family gathered. She loved Mother Renee, and she had once been close to everyone — spent a lot of time there for Sunday dinners and holiday celebrations, but since the separation, things were obviously not the same. The strains of the marriage brought strain to all the relationships. There had been a lot of drama. The Wooten clan, always close, had heard one side of it. They had watched with great concern the struggles of my father and blamed her for at least some of it. With his death, those feelings only intensified. Some in the family, unable to accept the enormity of suicide, posited that someone else must have done it — some crooked business partner, some disgruntled investor … or maybe someone interested in her. Of course, I did not know any of that then. At that moment, I still thought he had died of arthritis.

Mama herself may not have known such imaginings existed — but she could feel the strain, the blame, I am sure. She likely blamed herself in some measure for his death and carried guilt with her as she drove up the once-familiar driveway that led to bittersweet memories and wishes that she could do it over again, change some things. For this young thirty-two-year-old woman, widowed in the most terrible and complicated way, the emotional pain of stepping into that old mill-village house must have been almost unbearable.

For me, it was the natural place to go, the place where I could hang out with my cousins. As an only child (and an only grandchild on my mother's side), I lived so much of my life in the presence of adults that to spend time with my cousins was often the highlight of my life. Water gun battles, roll-to-the-bat, kick-the-can, capture-the flag — I loved all the running and rowdiness. I was the youngest of six — four boys, two girls. They mostly treated me as special (except for the time they took me snipe-hunting in the nearby church cemetery). Everybody called me "Little Jimmy," which is a hoot nowadays, considering how much bigger I am than anyone on that side of the family — but it is a term of endearment that connected me to my father and still brings a smile when my only living cousin Renee uses it.

Renee — a year-and-a-half older than me and the cousin to

whom I was probably always the closest — is the one who spilled the beans to me about the true nature of my father's death. It was unintentional, and she was horrified when she realized she did. She carried (and still carries) the kindness and general goodness that characterized her namesake, our grandmother Irene. Renee was trying to be positive and encouraging, repeating what she had obviously heard from others — but her words were a bombshell that exploded my psyche.

We were all playing in the backyard. It is strange how children can step away from harsh realities and get lost in play, a remarkable coping mechanism. If you had seen me running and laughing that day, you would never have guessed what was being talked about inside by the adults, nor the processing that was going on within the hearts and minds of each of us kids at play. At some point, during the games, we must have spoken to each other of what we were thinking and feeling, because Renee, trying to make some sense of it all, trying to find or provide some comfort, said, "The doctors said it was probably for the best, that the damage to the brain was so severe he would have been a vegetable if he had survived." "Stunned" is the word that comes to mind. It was as if everything stopped. "His brain?" I asked. "I thought he died of arthritis." Renee had a look of terror on her face. I am not sure what else was said, if she or one of the older boys explained, or if anyone explained. I am not sure I knew at that moment, by explanation or intuition, that he had shot himself — but I realized I had been lied to. I recognized that everyone else knew something I did not know.

I went screaming into the house. I think Renee did, too. I tore through the crowd of grown-ups, looking for my mother, crying and shouting, "What happened to my daddy?" It must have been harrowing for everyone there, especially for my mother. It was certainly not the way she would have wanted me to learn this truth that she had been unable to find the words to tell me, that nobody knew how to tell me. She cried. She held me as I sobbed. She tried to tell me, as gently as she could, what he had done and how hard it was to tell me, how hard it was for everybody to understand. Renee was crying, too — she needed comforting, too. She came to us and said she was so sorry, she did not mean to say something she should not have, and my mother told her it was okay, that it was not her fault. That was true. It was a secret that should not have been — and could never have been — kept.

It makes a difference how your loved one dies. It is excruciating to lose someone central in your life under any circumstance — but it makes a difference how it happens. And it matters exceedingly how you learn the details of that death, as hard as it may be for whoever has to tell you.

Secrets are never good. They can seldom be kept.

One day I learned that I lost my dad. I was heartbroken. The next day I learned he died violently, by his own hand — and I was the last to know. I was devastated and confused. I would have been devastated and confused no matter how or when I was confronted with the news. But because I was the last to know, I also felt foolish. It was MY father, and everybody knew but me. Somehow, it made the stigma worse if no one could speak of it to me.

Dr. Edward Dunne, a respected clinical psychologist

and author of *Suicide and Its Aftermath: Understanding and Counseling the Survivors* (and also a suicide survivor himself) wrote: "Children eventually find out the truth, and often under circumstances where they are given little support, like hearing the news from a schoolmate or a relative … . Why betray the trust of children, when they have already been betrayed by one adult? Children should learn from the experience that not all adults will abandon you or let you down."[8]

Long after I grew up, barely three months or so into a new pastorate, I got the call that a beloved longtime member and deacon of that church had, in the early morning hours, taken his own life at his place of business in much the same manner as my father had. It was devastating for a lot of people, and a disturbing flashback for me as I hurried to the family's home — the chaos of people scurrying everywhere, not knowing what to say or do; the strange combination of stunned silence and knowing whispers and stifled weeping and open wailing; the air permeated with unspoken questions and unremitting dread.

One of the daughters was in a bedroom, away from everyone else, struggling not only with the shock of her own grief but the burden of what to tell her sons. She was a sweet and sensitive soul, and her boys were extremely close to their grandfather. I shared with her my experience, and, as gently as I could, I told her how important it was that they hear the truth from someone they looked up to, someone they trusted, that they would hear it soon enough anyway. She said that made sense to her, and she was grateful.

Years later, she told me she did not divulge to them at that time the circumstances of their grandfather's death and tried to hide it from them, but it was not long before someone else revealed it. She knew it was a mistake and thought maybe it caused some problems.

I get the hesitancy. I really do. I recognize in my own mother's qualms that there was love behind it. I understand that it is hard to speak of such enormity when you are stunned and heartbroken yourself. But I wish someone close could have sat down and told me, cried with me, told me they did not understand either, and that it was normal to feel the way I felt.

Nobody did.

Chapter 14

ON A HILL FAR AWAY: THE FUNERAL

I have learned as I have moved from one pastorate to another in five different settings that each community has its own unique rituals and traditions when it comes to honoring the deceased and comforting the bereaved. In my rural Kentucky pastorate, quite a bit of time usually passed between the death and the funeral. Someone from the family or friends sat with the body at the mortuary around the clock, or at least for as long as the mortuary was open. It seemed interminable to me. In South Carolina, a two- or three-day interval is more the norm.

Of course, suicide is not the norm. Everything from autopsies and investigations to shattered emotions and disoriented thinking and unrelenting shame work against the standard routine. One would presume that it would take extra time to work through such issues, but it seems my father's service was almost as sudden as his death. This may explain, in part, why the whole thing is a blur to me.

Daddy died at three o'clock on Monday afternoon in Greenville. My mother was not even back in Laurens until around five o'clock in the evening. The newspaper article that appeared on the front page of the Wednesday morning, June 20 edition not only told of his apparent suicide, but it also included his obituary and the announcement that the funeral would be conducted later that same day at 5:00 p.m. at Kennedy Mortuary. All of that is highly irregular. A tantalizing news story combined with an obituary! A funeral announced on the day it occurs! A 5:00 p.m. service! I have never in my life been to another five o'clock funeral, and I have been to more funerals than just about anyone I know. No time for visitation prior to the service.

I guess maybe somebody chose that option considering the circumstances, but through the years I have attended visitations for families of suicide victims. The need for support and contact is just as great, or more so, in those circumstances. For some reason, the choices for my father's funeral seem "off" to me. They felt intuitively "off" even then, like it was rushed or was not being addressed properly, but it was a vague feeling. I had nothing then to base it on. Now, as one who has been involved in planning and conducting hundreds of funerals, I am somewhat fascinated at trying to understand just how the societal influences and familial circumstances came to bear on this experience.

I recall a feeling of isolation, despite what seemed like the whole town being there. Most of what I remember is sitting in the family car when we drove up, and, while we waited to leave for the cemetery, looking at all the people, trying to pick out folks I knew. The inside of the mortuary is not that big. There was a sensationalism to the story. He was young and had been involved in a lot of things. So, despite not a lot of notice, there was an overflow crowd of people gathered outside the mortuary, covering the lawn, and lining the sidewalks as we arrived, but I never got to talk to any of them that I recollect. I am not sure I wanted to talk to anybody. I was lost in my own thoughts.

When we got to the funeral home, we were ushered in through the front door. To my right, I saw the casket and felt — what would be the word — dread, fear, sadness? No word will do. Since there had been no visitation, that was my first time there. No one offered for me to go to the casket. I certainly did not ask to do so. Whatever I saw was from a distance, and I only passed through that room briefly on my way to a back room where the family sat during the service, away from prying eyes.

In my memory, the casket was open, and I could see something white — what appeared to be a bandage where his head lay in repose. I can see it clear as day, but I have always harbored some doubt as to the reality of that memory. Would they open a casket in such a circumstance? Would the wound allow it? Would a bandage be placed there? That seems unlikely. I asked my cousin Renee if she remembered seeing my father, and if so, did she see a bandage. She was not sure — thought she saw him in the casket, but no bandage. I have determined that the image in my head was a picture of what I was afraid I would see, not what I actually did see, when I glanced at that casket as I hurried through the room — a dreaded imagining that became almost tangible to me. Not long ago, I retrieved records from the mortuary. They did not tell me much I did not know, except this: "No open casket."

I have learned as an adult how important it is in the grief process to view the body of the loved one who has died, that somehow this makes the death real and keeps the mind from playing the denial game that cannot quite accept the actuality. With a violent death that damages the body, such a viewing is often untenable. The trauma of seeing is more damaging than the unsettled yearnings of not seeing. Still, for me, the repercussions of not ever seeing my father's body were evident in the months following his death.

I specifically recall a dream I had a little more than a year later, after my mother had remarried and we had moved to Aiken. In the dream, my stepfather had died and was in the bedroom where he and my mother slept. She was crying and insisting that I needed to go and see him, and I was resisting. We stood at the door, gazing in. I could see the form of his body under the covers, but the lamp on the bedside table obscured his head. She kept gently nudging me to step forward, and slowly I took small steps, until I was close enough to look upon his face — but when I gazed down, it was not my stepfather but my father's face I saw. I woke up screaming and drenched with sweat. I think that dream stemmed, in large measure, from a funeral experience at which I never saw for myself that my father was gone.

One of the unique patterns of Laurens funerals, at least in the past, was the penchant to have multiple ministers to speak at the service — never just one, often three, and I have participated with four. With my father, it was two: Alvin Boone, the longtime pastor who had baptized my mother at Lucas Avenue, and Giles Lewis, the young minister at the Episcopal church my father and I had been attending. As one who has presided at funerals as a minister myself, I look back with sympathy for the challenge they faced. It would be tough to find the right words to say in such a situation, and apparently with little time. I am sure they made a valiant attempt, and Giles Lewis played a tremendous role in caring for me and shaping my life in the aftermath — but I do not remember a word they said that day. My lasting impression is that I was disappointed that no one captured the essence of who my father was, that the tragic circumstances of his death overwhelmed a broader recollection of the person he was. When I became a minister, I determined that the uniqueness of every person, made in the image of God and valued as God's inimitable creation, demanded my best attempt to capture and celebrate that distinctiveness, no matter the circumstances of that person's death or life. That decision had its roots in my wishing that someone would have rendered that service to me.

When the words were spoken, the hymns were sung and the prayers were offered, we made our way back to the family car and waited. It seems like there is a lot of waiting at funerals. I looked out the window, picking out faces of people who had been a part of his life and mine. I remember the flowing robes of my Episcopal minister and the burdened look upon his face as he descended the steps. One of the pallbearers was my father's old friend in whose wedding I had been the ring bearer, the man who would become my deacon and *my* friend. I specifically remember seeing my father's young co-worker from Gastonia — surprised that news had traveled that far so quickly, and oddly comforted that he had come all that way. I shouted out to my mother, "There's Bunky! There's Bunky!" She looked but did not know who she was looking for. Nobody knew who Bunky was, but me. And before I could get a window down or get out of the car, he was gone, dispersed among the folks hurrying for their cars as we prepared to process to the cemetery. I never saw him again.

We followed the hearse around the Square, past the savings and loan where my mother worked, past his old office, past the places where I used to hang out with him — just a few blocks to the city cemetery where his family would, one by one, join him in the years not too distant. He was the first. It was the Laurens City Cemetery, not the one in Watts Mill. Mama would be buried in Woodlawn, surrounded by my stepfather's family, not far from Carlton, and, eventually, further up the hill, Granny. It has always struck me as emblematic of the brokenness and dysfunction of my family that my parents are buried alone in separate cemeteries.

I must have gone to the graveside for the committal, though I do not remember it specifically. That is what I would be expected to do. Yet, I have some inclination to believe that I stayed in the limo with the air-conditioning going during the committal service, though I am not certain why. (I am not even sure cars had air-conditioning in 1962, though fancy funeral home limos would be among the first.) Perhaps I had just had as much as I could emotionally take. Perhaps it was a small act of rebellion or protest, an act of resentment at the circumstance I found myself in. Perhaps my mother just offered or suggested it. The reason I believe that I did not go to the graveside, or at least came back to the car soon, is that I distinctly recall being alone in the family car for some time, watching the people as they stood around the grave and as they made their way past me. I not only was alone, but I also *felt alone.* My impression is that the windows of the limo were tinted (though I am not sure they tinted windows then either), as if I could see the people passing by more clearly than they could see me. I did not want them to see me. I did not want them to stop, and yet I kind of did want them to stop. And while I was grateful for those whose presence said that my father's life mattered, I watched them and knew that my grief was infinitely deeper than theirs. They were going back to the same lives they had been living. I had no idea what my life was going to be.

One of them did stop. It was Pete Mitchell, the white-haired owner of the café on the Square where my father would take me for breakfast or for my Dr. Pepper fix. He tapped on the window, and I opened the door. He leaned in and patted my arm. He spoke with an accent — Greek or Italian, I am not sure — but I remember exactly what he said: "Jimmy, your daddy was a good man … and you a good boy. You going to be okay." Those simple, heartfelt words were both the eulogy and the word of hope I needed to hear. They have stayed with me when almost nothing else from that day has.

Years later when my own son Grant was born and we lived through his preschool years in Laurens, while my wife worked at her part-time job, I would carry him with me on some of my errands, as my father did with me. Occasionally, on a pretty day, we would take a lunch and have a picnic beside his grandfather's resting place. I would sit on the grassy hill overlooking the Little River that winds through the valley below, and I would watch as my boy scooted all around the headstones and tumbled in the open grassy areas. He was too little to understand or even remember, but I would tell him about his grandfather — more for my sake than his, I guess. I would tell him of how my daddy taught me how to swim like I did for him, and how my father took me to the Myrtle Beach Pavilion to ride the same carnival rides I would take him to ride, how we would play golf together like I did with my old man.

In some ways, old Pete Mitchell was right, I remember thinking. I was okay. But in some ways, I wondered if I will ever be over it — not just the grief, not just the yearning for my father to know my son, and now my daughter. It is those unanswered questions that still lurk just beneath, rising to the surface from time to time, when I least expect it. It is those unresolved feelings that have left their imprint on my personality and my psyche, and continue to plague me in ways that I recognize — and, I am sure, in ways that I do not.

My father used to sing of the day when his "trophies at last (he) lay down." Tucked away in a closet in my home are the few trophies he laid down when he died: his notary public stamp or seal, his Hejaz fez (and the one for his lady, my mother), a golf trophy, the Father's Day card and poem, a couple of other small trinkets. As precious as they are, they sadden me to see how little he left behind, the potential unrealized. In some strange way, I think I have carried the burden of his unfulfilled potential — the need to make amends, and the fear I will not measure up either.

My father used to sing of a cross on a hill far away — a cross that held the promise of sins forgiven and the hope of a home beyond this life. Now he is buried high on that hill in the town where he lived and died, and I pray that by God's good grace, his hopes have been fulfilled and he is finally at peace. It is peace in this life that I seek as well, as we all do, and I cannot help but ponder if that peace is a little harder to find when you are the Suicide's Son.

BIG
Opening Dance
at Curry's Swiming Pool
Friday Night, February 27, 1925.

This is our Big Opening Dance, so let everybody come out and have a good time. This dance is absolutely

"FREE"

Come and Bring Your Friends

There will be a dance every Friday night

Dancing at Curry's Lake
Bands · Player Piano · Piccolo · Jukebox
Square Dancing · Shaggi...

For nearly half of the twentieth century, Curry's Lake was the recreational and entertainment venue in Laurens County, South Carolina, for the young and old alike. Jim Wooten and Colleen Willard dated there often. (Courtesy of Sara Jane Armstrong)

With dreams and hopes for the future, Colleen and Jim Wooten made their son, little Jimmy, feel like the center of attention.

In less than ten years after this photo, both my daddy, Jim Wooten (left) and my maternal grandfather, Carlton Willard (right) were dead from suicide.

I am standing at the recent burial place of my grandfather, Carlton Willard, on Easter Sunday, 1962, just two months before my father's death.

Happy Father's Day

Dear Daddy,
I love you more than words can say,
I love you in every kind of way.
I enjoy being with you, Even when I'm sad and blue.

Love,
Jimmy

I still have the card and the poems I wrote my daddy the day before his suicide, Father's Day, 1962. They were among the few items still in his possession that were kept and passed on to me.

In a childhood portrait, my mother, the young Colleen Willard, sports the same Dutch-boy bobbed haircut that the actress Colleen Moore made famous. Circa 1934.

*My mother secured
a job at WLBG, the
local Laurens, South
Carolina, AM radio
station, and as a
bookkeeper at the
Buick dealership.
She was smart and
hardworking, never at
a loss for employment,
even when her journey
took her to new cities.*

*My parents had a wide circle of friends and spent lots
of time at the Lake Greenwood summer homes of some
of them. My mother's work owned a place at Pawleys
Island, South Carolina, and multiple families would
attend house parties there in the summer. I still enjoy
South Carolina coastal vacations with my family today.*

In 1974, not long before my mother was diagnosed with the illness that would take her life at the tender age of forty-five, Helen Reddy recorded "You and Me Against the World," a song that always makes me think of the two of us, especially after my father's death. In it, a mother sings to her child of how the two of them together can get through anything the world throws at them — and even when one of them is no longer there, their memory will help the other carry on.

PART II

JIMMY:
LIVING IN THE SHADOW,
SEARCHING FOR THE LIGHT

Chapter 15

THE QUESTION … AND OTHER QUESTIONS

"You might be looking for reasons, but there are no reasons."
— Nina LaCour, *Hold Still*

In 1961, the same year my grandfather Willard swallowed a
bottle of pills in Modesto, California, and ended his life, a little
further north in Ketchum, Idaho, the legendary author Ernest
Hemingway took a shotgun and did the same. Nobody much
took note of the former. The whole literary world, and much of
the rest of the Western globe, fixated on the latter. Speculation
was rampant. Was it premeditated, or just a sudden moment of
despair — or was it even intentional in the first place? The local
priests, for some reason, resisted calling it a suicide.

The author's granddaughter, actress Mariel Hemingway,
pondered this legacy after the suicide of her model/actress sister
Margaux (the seventh suicide in that family tree). She was also
moved by the death of comedian Robin Williams when she wrote:
"There is a quote that's circulating, something he (Williams) said in
character in a film: 'Suicide is a permanent answer to a temporary
problem.' Personally, I think that's too pat. The truth is scarier,
because it reveals something more profound about the ripple

effect of suicides, how they leave behind a lifetime of wondering, doubting, and rationalizing, a lifetime of slowly coming to the understanding that there is no definitive understanding, and there never will be. Suicide is a permanent question."[9]

A permanent question … yes!

Inevitably, whenever someone hears that my father committed suicide, the conversation will soon include the question: "Why did he do it?" "Why" is always THE question. Inquiring minds want to know, as if you can find some neat, tidy answer that renders such an act understandable. It is the question those who are left behind struggle with for the rest of their lives. In the end, you can cite factors, but you can never truly explain it. From my perspective, that is a major reason the grief is so hard to process completely.

For everyone who, in facing adversity, pain, heartache, shame or financial hardship chooses such a dire "solution," you can point to hundreds, probably thousands, who face the same general circumstances who find other ways of coping. Of course, we know a lot more about mental illness and depression, clinically speaking, than we did in 1962, but clinical insights do not fully explain or satisfy.

"Why" is always THE question that remains unanswered.

I can give you factors that I believe contributed to my father's suicide. He suffered great physical pain, all his life, from a crippling case of rheumatoid arthritis. As a child, he was bedridden at times — to the point that his absences forced him to repeat at least one year in grade school. As an adult, he often walked with a limp when the arthritis flared up. I remember, as a preschooler cuddled up beside him as he steered the car on a Sunday afternoon drive through the country, accidentally bumping his knee and him screaming with pain. It was a rare reaction. He seldom complained. But I know he suffered.

My dad drank, and alcohol is a depressant. I never knew his drinking to cause him to miss work or to produce any major crisis (at least until the end), but I realize now that he was certainly an alcoholic, numbing his pain (both physical and psychic) with beer and liquor. In reflection, I stand amazed at the number of times my memory of my father includes him drinking. It clearly worsened in the closing weeks of his life. It showed, even to a child.

His marriage was in trouble. My parents were separated and (as I have written) it was a lot more complicated than that. Another romantic relationship had just ended, not by his choice. His personal life was in turmoil, as was his professional life. A major business reversal, with severe financial and legal ramifications — coupled with what he felt was betrayal by partners — shook his self-esteem and threatened his reputation. The anxiety must have been unbearable.

As I recently read *Night Falls Fast: Understanding Suicide*, these words jumped out at me: "We know for example, a great deal about underlying conditions that predispose an individual to kill himself — heredity, severe mental illness, an impulsive or violent temperament — and *we know, too, that there are some events or circumstances in life that interact in a particularly deadly way with these predisposing vulnerabilities: romantic failures or upheavals; economic or job setbacks; confrontations with the law; terminal or debilitating illnesses; situations that cause great shame, or are perceived as such; the injudicious use of alcohol or drugs.*"[10]

My father experienced ALL of these events and circumstances in a compressed amount of time.

In many ways, 1962 brought a perfect storm of troubles into his life. Beyond all these struggles, he also had an untimely example of suicide within the family that surely had an impact upon him. In late October of 1961, Carlton Willard, my mother's father, took pills to end his life. (His youngest brother, Walter, had taken his own life at an early age, so Carlton himself had lived with that example as well.) Carlton died in faraway California while writing a letter to my mother as he drifted from consciousness, the letter unfinished, even as his life at fifty-one years of age was unfinished. Though they were different in many ways (my grandfather tall and temperamental, my father shorter and even-keeled), they had an appreciation for one another and got along on the rare occasions they were together.

My grandfather's body was brought back to Laurens for burial, and our house was the place where family and old acquaintances came to pay their respects. My parents were separated then, but my father was there as the house was full of people. I remember him being ill-at-ease, and I particularly picture him standing away from everyone else, pensively thumbing through the pages of the "In Memoriam" book placed in our living room by the funeral home for guests to sign. Was he ill-at-ease because it was awkward to be there when they were separated, or just because he was uncomfortable in the face of death and grief? Or was he thinking other thoughts, darker thoughts?

I cannot help but think a seed was planted. Jamison writes, "The contagious quality of suicide, or the tendency for suicides to occur in clusters, has been observed for centuries and is at least partially responsible for some of the ancient sanctions against suicide." One suicide can encourage another. "The tendency for suicide to incite imitation … is persistent," Jamison reiterates.[11]

Clearly, a tsunami of factors overwhelmed my father.

Older people used to say to me, as a means of comfort, "Well, he just wasn't in his right mind." Obviously, that is true. His depression was severe and evident, but was his "mind" always predisposed to depression? Not in my memory. Was he temperamental and impulsive? My grandfather Willard fit that bill better than my father. Was there a pattern of suicide in his family lineage? Maybe some eccentricity, but no suicide to which anyone could point. This issue of a predilection of deep-rooted mental illness in my father, always assumed, would become one of the big questions for me in adulthood.

If you asked for my vote on THE question of "Why," I would give top-billing to chronic alcoholism made acute by overwhelming circumstances — but, then again, those circumstances were mostly the result of choices he made and actions he took.

In the end, "Why" remains unknowable — and, as a child, it was not the most important question I had anyway.

Chapter 16

Was I Not Enough? — The Question of Worth

"When people kill themselves, they think they are ending the pain, but all they're doing is passing it on to those they leave behind." — Jeannette Walls, *Half Broke Horses*

For me, as a ten-year-old, my father's suicide raised a far more personal and pressing question than "Why?" It stirred somewhere in the depths of my being, searing yet ineffable. If I could have articulated the question that cut to the bone, it would have been this: Wasn't I enough to live for?

I did not fully grasp all the adult issues that were happening around me. I could not analyze the factors that would lead to such a decision. I did not have some academic understanding of the pervasiveness of suicide and the destructive power of untreated mental illness. Those issues would not have mattered to me anyway. All I knew was that the man who I looked up to, the man who spent so much time with me and told me he loved me and made me feel that I was the most important person in the world to him, this man who was the most significant man in my life would rather die than go on living with me.

Suicide feels, to those closest and left behind, like the ultimate rejection. It is a willful desertion — not unlike the act of abandoning one's family, except worse. It is a violent, permanent severing of a relationship. How could it not have a profound effect on the sense of self-worth of those who found value in being loved by the one who now chose to leave them to fend for themselves and face a life made more challenging by that choice? This is especially so for a child, whose image of himself or herself is in a critical, formative stage.

I would imagine it is difficult for anyone to accurately assess the health of his own self-image, his sense of self-worth. I know it is for me. On the one hand, following my father's death, from adolescence into adulthood, I have stepped out time and again in making myself vulnerable: running for student government offices in every school I attended, from junior high through seminary; auditioning for dramatic productions as a youth and as an adult; trying out for sports teams; pursuing a doctoral degree; leading countless organizations in seeking to achieve goals; standing in a pulpit and speaking Sunday after Sunday; even writing this book and daring to publish it. In all these cases (and more), there is significant risk of rejection and failure. I have experienced both success and failure in all these endeavors. (I think Lewis Grizzard is the one who said, "Winning never feels as good as losing feels bad!" I would agree.) I would have to think that it takes a certain amount of ego-strength to take such risks, and to bounce back from a defeat and try again. I saw that ego-strength modeled in my mother, and I attribute much of whatever confidence or deter-mination I have to her example and her support, particularly in the aftermath of my father's death. All in all, I think I have known more success than failure, and on one level I am proud of (and somewhat surprised by) my accomplishments.

Yet, on the other hand, none of the successes ever seem to satisfy. No matter the affirmation or the achievement, I always have a nagging feeling that I do not measure up, an unreasonable reaction that I should have done better, an underlying and uneasy sensation of unworthiness. It is like I am looking for something I cannot find.

Early in my seminary education, I was assigned a field placement to serve as a volunteer chaplain five hours a week in Louisville General Hospital. I had just turned twenty-two, right out of college, with no pastoral training or experience. It was trial by fire. As a downtown hospital of a large city, the cases there were varied and intense: death in the ER, terminal patients on the cancer ward, poverty-stricken unwed mothers with complicated lives on the maternity ward, people facing surgeries of varying degrees of seriousness. I threw myself into that assignment, worked beyond my assigned hours, tried to make whatever difference one can make in such a brief time, but I (understandably) felt overwhelmed and inadequate. That is part of the education. Most, if not all, people would feel similarly.

For me, the more enlightening insight arose from the closing evaluation by my supervisor, who was one of the main chaplains at the hospital. He was a man not given to warmth of personality — aloof, cold, clinical, frustrating for me to try to connect with. Overall, the evaluation was positive, although I (typically) do not remember any of the good things he said, only the one disturbing comment: "Jim, you have an unhealthy need for affirmation, and if you don't get ahold of it, it will trip you up." I did not like hearing it (after all, it was not particularly affirming), but he had me pegged. Even then, we both saw the roots of the problem in my father's suicide. I am not sure I have ever gotten "ahold of it," and it *has* tripped me up along the way — at least emotionally.

Of course, everyone has insecurities. The battle for a sense of self-worth is a hard-fought contest for most people, and most of those who struggle with it have never lost someone to suicide. But for those who have, I can almost bet that it was a blow to their sense of self-worth that has had repercussions over the course of their lives. It is not an excuse — but it is an explanation, at least in part.

Somewhere, in the deepest recesses of my being, a question still lingers from my father's suicide that no amount of affirmation or achievement can quite alleviate: Was I not enough to live for?

Chapter 17

What Could I Have Done? — The Question of Guilt

"No amount of guilt can change the past, and no amount of worry can change the future." — Umar Ibn Al-Khattaab

I hesitate to cite Woody Allen after the recent televised treatments of his daughter's allegations of his perverse actions and the ensuing notoriety, but he has a funny quote from one of his early comedy routines. Allen built a career on making fun of his neurotic feelings and behavior. "When we played softball," he quipped, "I'd steal second base, feel guilty, and go back."[12]

Those words came back to me as I recalled a long-ago lunch with two fellow ministers, friends from my seminary days, at a restaurant in Atlanta. We were there for a convention. The waitress came to our table. Something about the way I placed my order made one of them say, "You are the only person I have ever heard sound like they are apologizing when they are ordering their food." We laughed. I said, "I sometimes feel guilty just taking up space on this earth," and it was not totally just a joke. From whence cometh such a feeling? I can think of one possibility.

Survivor's guilt is a strange phenomenon, a totally irrational yet all-too-common reaction to traumatic death. Many stories were written about it in the wake of the tragedy of 9/11. People who survived the Twin Towers' bombing and rescue personnel who lost co-workers suffered persistent mental and emotional stress, in which they felt guilty for surviving when others did not. Combat veterans suffering from PTSD often deal with such guilt. From what I can tell, the trauma of suicide almost always produces a similar guilt reaction in those who are left behind — maybe not as severe, but it can be just as relentless. "What could I have done differently? What should I have said, or not said? Why didn't I notice?"

In one church I served as pastor, a beloved Sunday School class leader took his own life at his workplace on a Monday. The day before, as the class shared prayer concerns, he said he had an "unspoken" request. It is not rare for someone to make such an appeal for some need for which they do not want to share private details. For years, to this day, someone will often say to me, "I should have asked after class what was going on," as if he would have told them; "I should have known," as if every unspoken request is of such dire desperation. Even for friends, not just family, the grief is unresolved — and the guilt, however irrational, stirs whenever the memory is called forth.

Not everyone expresses it openly, but most feel it. We feel responsible for the ones we love — and when something bad happens to them, it is only natural that we wonder what we could have done differently to alleviate their pain, get them help, treat them differently. Guilt or regret is a natural part of the grief cycle in any instance. When someone we love has grown so disenchanted as to willfully take his or her life, the potential for that guilt or regret is surely exacerbated.

Yet, Kay Redfield Jamison reminds us that "Love, success, and friendship are not always enough to counter the pain and destructiveness of severe mental illness,"[13] and few of us are equipped to adequately recognize or deal with such. This was even more true in 1962 than now. Advances have been made in psychiatric treatment, and a broader openness and understanding of psychiatric issues exists these sixty years later — but it remains true that the problem with suicide is that it is an act of the will. It is not an accident that befalls someone, but a choice they make.

I do not remember ever feeling any conscious guilt about my father's death. I was a child, after all, hardly responsible for major decisions or actions that would have affected him. The only pang of regret I have ever specifically pinpointed was my choice not to play golf with him that Sunday morning when all the chaos was going on. I do not think that would have made any difference in the choice he made, but I still sometimes wish I had gone with him.

For the adults, it may have been different. My mother never spoke of any guilt she felt, but I know she must have experienced it. She bore her burdens alone, unexpressed, stoic. The morning "showdown" at our house was horrific — but it was she who reached out to him in the afternoon, she who expressed her love for him and a desire to make things work. Still, before that, words spoken or unspoken, deeds done or left undone — there is always something we wish we could take back or do over, and I am confident that in the brokenness of their relationship, that was especially so. My Aunt Martha spoke of wishing she had known what to say when he called her from that pay phone.

When something as devastating and inconceivable and hurtful

as suicide happens, it is hard to accept and process. There is the tendency to look for someone to blame. Guilt is the inclination to turn anger inward and to blame oneself, even when there is no conscious reason to do so. A sensitive soul — prone to take upon himself or herself the burdens of others and unwilling to hold their loved one responsible — may carry that burden a long time and never even recognize it. How can you be angry with the one whose pain was so intense it took his life? So you bury that anger, and it does its dirty work down deep. Sometimes it surges forth in self-destructive bursts — fits of temper, impulsive actions that undermine your relationships and threaten your sense of well-being. More often, it seems to ooze out over the long haul, permeating your life in unhealthy ways that just compound your guilt — addictive behaviors and incessant worry.

It is not an excuse — but this unresolved anger aimed inward, this unwarranted guilt may be an explanation for some of the ways we limit and punish ourselves. If guilt is only a conscious awareness of failing the one we have lost, then maybe guilt has not been my problem. If, however, guilt is seen as unresolved anger turned inward, it may be a different story. It is hard for me to admit anger at my father, but I can certainly see where the hurt from his actions has impacted my life in negative ways.

Chapter 18

What Should *They* Have Done? — The Question of Blame

"When you blame and criticize others, you are avoiding some truth about yourself" — Deepak Chopra

Of course, not everyone struggles with guilt. Some, in their anger and bewilderment, turn it outward, look for others to blame. I sensed some of this within the family toward my mother. "If she had treated him differently," they reasoned, "he would never have done what he did." Maybe so. If they had paid more attention to the signs of his unraveling, maybe they could have gotten him some help. The blame game has room for many.

I audibly heard this tendency to blame regarding the business associates whom they (probably correctly) perceived as "crooks" who used my father and his connections in our town to gain entrée to get to other people's money. Some even hypothesized that his death was murder, not suicide. The truth they were avoiding, the truth they could not face, was the fact that my father's actions were his own. He chose his associates. He chose his manner of death.

The reason they could not face that fact, lay, at least in part, in the inevitable loss of the ideal with which they perceived my father. He was a bright star in the family — the only boy, lively, witty, and charismatic. My cousin Joe used to tell me that my father had a presence about him that belied his physical stature — that when he was in the room, attention immediately moved to him. It warmed my heart to think that my cousin saw him the way I saw him. Others shared that perception.

How does one reconcile such a perception with the somber and dismaying reality that Jim failed in business, failed in marriage, and was not strong enough to handle the vicissitudes of the life he crafted? You soften the blow of the loss of the ideal by finding someone else to blame or criticize, and in so doing you avoid not only the truth about Jim, but also the truth about your own misjudgment. You temper your disillusionment with him, and with yourself, by shifting the focus to someone else.

This is an all-too-human response practiced countless times in the face of deep disappointment. It is a defense mechanism to protect oneself against disillusionment. I have encountered it time and again in my ministry — people who cannot face the truth about themselves or others. They create false narratives and deflect to a scapegoat to protect the image others have of them, and, more importantly, the image they have of themselves. It is easy to see it in others, not so easy to see it in ourselves. One of the reasons I remember so clearly the accusations against my father's business partners is because those accusations eased my troubled psyche and protected some portion of my image of my father.

Yet, one can only be disillusioned if what one believed was an illusion in the first place. This book is an attempt to be delivered, as much as possible, from any illusions about my father — his life or his death — and about the people and the circumstances around him, and the ways his story has affected my life. Blame gets in the way of such a quest. It camouflages the truth. Blame is a waste of time.

I could blame my father, but that would obscure the goodness that was within him and the vibrancy of our relationship, as brief as it was. It would also minimize the reality and impact that mental illness so often plays. If he had a physical malady, a heart attack, would I blame him for that? I could blame my mother, but that would negate the struggle I saw in her to hold on to her marriage, a thirty-two-year-old who grew up in a fractured family of her own. That would only add to her burden. Was it Papa's fault for setting a poor example or maybe some perceived leniency in Mother Renee? The girlfriend? How can one blame another person for stepping away from a relationship that was built on the wrong reasons? Though I cannot posit any merit in the business partners, they did not dictate my father's actions — and who knows the backstory that shaped their lives and decisions.

Nobody wanted anything like his suicide to happen. Nobody saw it coming. Pretty much everybody was devastated by it.

No one in the story was perfect. All of us had things we could have handled better. Human beings can be frail and fallible, particularly when faced with trials, sorrows and disappointments that overwhelm them.

How do we acknowledge that frailty, in others and in ourselves, without blame or excuse? How do we share our confusion and feelings of inadequacy in a community of grief and help each other through it? Blaming is counterproductive.

What should *they* have done? Given who they were and the circumstances they were in, I am not sure there was any one act that would have altered the course of events in those final days and weeks.

The main thing I wish they would have done is the one thing that has kept this book from being written for five decades, the one thing I wish I had done sooner. I wish they — and I — had talked about it.

Chapter 19

SHALL WE TALK ABOUT IT? — THE QUESTION OF SHAME

"Suicide is not a blot on anyone's name; it is a tragedy."
— Kay Redfield Jamison, *Night Falls Fast: Understanding Suicide*

Two months after my father's death, school started back — my first day of fifth grade. It had been a whole summer since I had seen most of my classmates. A lot had happened since we were last together. I was a different person.

One of my first encounters was with a kid named Danny — not one of my closest friends, more an acquaintance, kind of rough around the edges. We were outside, before school began. I don't remember how the conversation started, but I remember his words: "Yeah, I saw in the paper that a James Wooten blew his brains out, and I wondered if it was you. Glad to see you back." I was stunned … angry at his insensitivity … "blew his brains out." I was mortified that, as I suspected, everybody knew — it was "in the paper." What I felt mostly was a stab of — what is the best word — shame.

It may be unfair, but you want to be proud of your father. I always had been. He was a nice-looking guy, stylish, popular in town. I liked how, when I would go to his office with him, we would go to the businesses around the Square — the café, the drug store, the barber shop, the men's store, all of them — and he engaged everybody in conversation, made them laugh. They were glad to see him come and sad to see him go. I liked how he played golf — with a little flair, like Arnie. Yet, standing on that playground, and in days to come, I had a sense of shame because of what he did (and a sense of guilt for feeling that way about him).

I am not sure if the shame and embarrassment was intuitive, or whether it was based on what I had learned from watching reactions of the adults in my life. It was probably both. Nobody referred to the circumstances. They talked around it, as if it were taboo. *It felt like it was taboo!* So, if someone has done something of which you cannot speak, surely it must be a shameful act.

Kay Redfield Jamison is correct that suicide is a tragedy, always a tragedy. But "not a blot on anyone's name," I am not so sure. Perhaps it *should not* be a blot, but I am afraid that it is. A stigma attaches to suicide — which, in one sense, just adds yet another indignity to someone who has already found his situation unbearable. Orson Scott Card, in his novel *Ender's Shadow,* has one of his characters make an insightful remark: "In my view, suicide is not really a wish for life to end … . It is the only way a powerless person can find to make everybody else look away from his shame. The wish is not to die, but to hide."[14]

This is an intriguing image to me. This man, who so desperately wanted to rise above his roots and to be seen as a success, already felt an inescapable stigma from the mess he had made of his life. His shame was so pervasive and the glare of scrutiny so unrelenting, he just wanted to hide, but he could find no place to do so. If the thought is correct, then death was not a desire to be rid of me, nor my mother, nor anyone else — not even a desire to be rid of life. It was simply the only way he could see that he could hide from his unbearable shame.

I could not hide. I had no idea who knew about the suicide — but if Danny did, I assumed everyone did.

Of all the ways I identify with my father, one of the strongest is an over-reactive fear of "looking bad." Of course, nobody wants to be seen in a negative light, but some people are driven not so much by a need to achieve some goal or acquire some possession for their own sake, but by the desire to measure up, to be validated. For my father, that meant escaping some personally perceived stigma of the mill village and forming a professional identity and associations with the "right" people. I have wondered how much of his self-image was shaped by his diminutive physical stature, and the crippling arthritis that made him bedridden for long stretches as a child — leaving him with a noticeable limp when it flared as an adult. Is that why he dressed so stylishly, went at the game of golf with such verve?

To be deemed a professional failure, to be judged with the "wrong people," to appear weak in any way would have been especially devastating and defeating to someone like him. The look that flashed across my father's face when his big, strong friend struck his arthritic knees to win that arm-wrestling match at the lake pops up in my mind. It was not anger. It was not just sadness at betrayal; it was shame. I see it now — he wanted to hide. In his mind, he "looked bad." His weakness was exposed. A minor episode, one might say, but very telling.

I played football when I was in high school. I came late to the game. I did not try out for the team until the ninth grade. Back then, I was very thin (hard to imagine now) and was one of the two or three lightest players on the team. Not blessed with either size or blazing speed, the main attributes I brought to the job were determination (nobody tried harder) and "good hands" (I could catch about anything that came my way). It was not enough to get off the second string and kickoff teams, but one week in my junior year I performed especially well in practice. I basked in the words of the coach, as I picked myself up after a tough catch over the middle: "Son, you are going to be a good receiver one day."

The next game, we were either winning big or losing big (I do not remember which) and some of my friends in the stands started a chant, which seemingly the whole stadium took up: "Put Wooten in! Put Wooten in!" I was embarrassed to be singled out like that. At some point, the coach came and asked if I was ready to go in. I froze. I shook my head and said, "I'm not sure I know the plays well enough," which may have been true but that was not the problem. I was afraid, especially with those people in the stands inordinately focused on me, that I would mess up and everyone would see. A spark of disappointment went across my coach's face, and he just nodded. To this day, that moment haunts me, because the opportunity for which I had worked so hard passed because I was afraid of "looking bad" in the eyes of my friends. I have no delusions of having become a star player — but I believe, in retrospect, I could have earned more playing time. Ironically, the shame of my timidity was far greater than any embarrassment that a mistake on the football field may have brought, and it lingers still.

Did I learn that fear of "looking bad" from him, or is it inherent in the way I am wired? Is it some mutation of his own insecurity passed down and finding a new expression in my life? My wife, Becky, and I have discussed how someone needs to do a sociological study not just of those who grew up in the mill village culture and moved on into professional lives, but also of the next generation. Does that next generation carry some of the need to prove themselves, some edge that those who grew up differently do not exhibit? In many instances, we believe we observe a pattern.

Whatever the source, I readily identify with the fear of being shamed that I discerned in my father. I cannot help but wonder if the manner of his death at such a formative moment in my development has contributed to it. I know I have spent an inordinate amount of energy not so much in trying to "look good," but in trying not to "look bad."

When I turned thirty-five, Becky had three of my high school buddies come to our home for a celebration cookout. I had not seen them in a while. In reminiscing with one of them about some of the crazy things we did growing up, I remarked, "I bet you are surprised that I became a minister." He laughed and said, "No, not really." I said, "I'm shocked, after all that stuff we did back then." He said, "Yeah, but you never seemed to enjoy it like the rest of us."

I have tried to process that observation. (Even the remark bothered me. What was wrong with me that he would remember me as different than everyone else?) Still, I have to admit his insight had merit. I probably did some things I did not really want to do because I did not want to look bad to my friends. More likely, I wanted to do them, but worried more than most about the shame (not punishment) I would experience and the disappointment I would cause if people who believed in me found out. While the fear of shame may have its place in keeping us on the straight and narrow, it is neither the most trustworthy moral imperative nor the surest path to sound decisions and a happy life.

I wish my father had known that. I am still working on it.

Chapter 20

Bitter or Better? — The Question of God

"You either get bitter or you get better. It is that simple. You either take what has been dealt to you and allow it to make you a better person, or you allow it to tear you down. The choice does not belong to fate, it belongs to you." — Josh Shipp

---

I have often contemplated why it is that some people, in the face of some great trauma or disappointment, become bitter — and some people do not. I have particularly wondered why I do not bear (and have never borne, in my memory) any discernible bitterness about my father's death — not toward him, not toward others (except maybe a hazy bitterness toward his business partners that I borrowed from grown-ups in my life), and certainly not toward God.

I have concluded that the roots of bitterness are often found in unrealistic expectations. I love going to Disney World. I went the first time not long after it opened, and I have taken my family there many times. A part of me buys into the hype — but every time I go, I see crying children and frenzied parents and weary people of all ages struggling to have a fun time in the "Happiest Place on Earth." If you think a trip to the Magic Kingdom is going to be *all* magic, you are in for a major disappointment. Disney is a wonderfully unique experience, and I would go back in a heartbeat — but it is not just as advertised. It can be hotter, more crowded, more expensive, more tiring, more challenging than the commercials would make you believe. I have heard some people say they will never go back. I know some people who want to live there. What makes the difference? Often, expectation makes the difference.

Unrealistic expectations spoil many of our experiences. When it comes to the big issues, the results can have long-lasting consequences. Marriages flounder, careers are abandoned, acquisitions disappoint — not because of anything inherently wrong about them, but because the realities do not meet anticipations. We thought it would be different than it is. Unrealistic expectations about the nature of life can be the same and can lead to a bitterness that colors the rest of life.

Going back to Disney, I have known people who grew up watching Walt's movies and say those movies shaped their expectations of how life would be — that, in the end, everyone would live happily ever after. Then, as time passed and problems came — some of them life-altering and serious — they have felt let down, even bitter. The cynic in me wants to remind them that not everyone lived happily ever after in those movies either: Old Yeller, Bambi's mother, Simba's daddy, and so on.

I have a friend who says he and his brothers grew up in a home that was like the old TV show, *Ozzie and Harriett*. His father was funny, his mother sweet, their marriage perfect, their problems minuscule. The boys all thought that was just how life was — but when they grew up, all three sons had marriages that failed for one reason or another. Shocked, they never considered such a possibility. They agreed that unrealistic expectations played a part in each of their stories. The lessons were hard. In some cases, the repercussions still linger — but each found a way to learn and move on, to get better.

There are no guarantees in life. I learned that lesson early. What amazes me, looking back, is how I processed it. The major players around me must have not only supported me, but also modeled a healthy response to a tragic disruption. My mother's strength shone through. I know she had support from the people at her work, people who helped her sort through the enormous financial and legal challenges my father's death left in its wake. I know from Granny (who may have harbored more than a little bitterness) that Daddy died with significant debt, which my mother had to pay off — some of it related to the business she pleaded with him not to undertake. Long after my mother died, I found old papers, correspondence tracking the ongoing court battle with the insurance company that sought to deny payment because it was a suicide. She never got all of it, and what she received did not cover his funeral costs. I was surprised, and maybe a little disappointed, at the people who came after money in his non-existent estate — and I was amazed at how my mother handled it all with such grace.

She never told me these things. I may have overhead some of it. What occurs to me is the fact that she never whined, never cast aspersions on my father or anyone in his family, never made me feel that somehow I had to prop her up emotionally. She went to work, made sure I was cared for, made life as normal as it could be. She kept going, and so did I. In her own way, Mother Renee did the same. They were the two people I looked to most for my cues in life — and as different as they were, I saw strength modeled for me in each of them.

Many people turn away from God, or even the idea of God, in response to a tragic loss. I get it. I totally understand it — but for some reason, I turned toward God. Just a few months before my father's death, I had made a commitment to Christ on my own in the wake of another tragic loss — my grandfather's death (Carlton). It was an intensely private and personal decision, made in the stillness of my parent's bedroom, looking at a picture of my grandfather on the wall when he was not much younger than I was at the time, and knowing how his life had turned out. I asked God to forgive me of my sins and to come into my life and help me be the person He wanted me to be.

Eventually, I shared this decision with my parents and my desire to join the church. I professed my faith and was baptized by affusion (pouring or sprinkling) as a believer in the sanctuary of the Church of the Epiphany on January 21, 1962. Despite their separation, both parents stood beside me as I took that step. I studiously and seriously attended the catechism classes that were taught and joyfully assumed the role of an acolyte. My heart was stirred. I found such meaning in helping to lead in worship: carrying the crucifer, lighting and extinguishing candles, setting the hymn numbers in the wooden display, serving as a kind of prompter, I guess — kneeling and rising at the appropriate time.

Just as I was loving God most and serving God best, the worst happened. The immediate aftermath of my father's death was a pivotal epoch in my spiritual journey, and I credit that young Episcopal minister and his little church for reaching out to me and not forgetting me. It was my father who took me there, and he was gone. It would have been easy to let me slip away.

Giles Lewis and his wife took me to a mountain retreat on a short vacation along with their young children. He continued to give me opportunities to serve as an acolyte, and I was a wise man in the Christmas pageant that year. (The older boys tried to get me to drink some of the wine they found back in the room where the robes were kept — but, typically, I did not want to "look bad," so I got out of it somehow.) Mother Renee and Mama came to see me in the pageant. I remember being grateful for their presence, and yet more keenly aware of my father's absence as I looked out at where they sat. I credit my mother for stepping up and making sure that influence was not interrupted in my life. It had not been her church, but she took me or made sure I was there. I had godparents who took their commitments seriously and reached out to me.

Through it all, God was very real to me. The prayers and the Scripture, the liturgy, the sermons comforted me. Though we moved away to Aiken, South Carolina, the next year when my mother remarried and we joined the First Baptist Church, a seed was planted that would one day lead me to ministry. Years later, when I was in my fifties, I tracked Giles Lewis down to tell him what he meant in my life. He had retired and moved back to South Carolina after serving in Texas. He visited my office, and I took him to lunch — and it was such a good feeling to be with him again. So often in ministry, you never know whether you made a difference, and I wanted him to know.

In my career, I have seen people become angry with God in the face of tragedy, and I understand it. Anger is a normal grief reaction, and it must be aimed somewhere. Often, it is at those to whom we are closest. After months of prayers and talks and visits in the home and in various hospitals with a young man in my church during his agonizing battle with brain cancer, he finally succumbed. I had become close to him and his family through that long ordeal. When he died, his wife turned and, with her fists, beat me in the chest and cried out, "You said he would be okay," before burying her head on my shoulder and weeping. The force of her anger startled me. I had never had it directed at me quite like that. Of course, I had never said that he would be okay. Somewhere, in her mind, in her denial, she thought that if we prayed hard enough and if she took care of him well enough, God would continue to spare him against all odds. She was angry at God, and I was God's representative.

Her anger at me quickly passed. I hope it did with God. Sometimes it does not. Acute anger metastasizes into a chronic bitterness that saps the joy and hope that is so essential for meaningful living and vibrant faith.

Such danger lurks in a shaky theology, in which we put unrealistic expectations on God and on life. I often remind myself and others that Jesus never tried to shield His followers from the realities of human existence or mislead them about the life of faith. On the night before His crucifixion, He told His disciples, "I have said these things to you, that in me you may have peace.

In this world you will have tribulation (trouble). But take heart, I have overcome the world" (John 16:33).

It is amazing how many times I quote that verse. I learned early, and have been reminded many times since, that there are troubles and tribulations in this world. That is the way life is. Jesus said so. But He also said we can take heart that He has overcome the world. There is a reality at work beyond what we always see in the moment.

The quote from Josh Shipp, a youth motivational speaker and author, that was cited at the beginning of this chapter is one that I came across a few years back. I posted it on my bulletin board because it resonated with me. "You either get bitter or you get better. It is that simple. You either take what has been dealt to you and allow it to make you a better person, or you allow it to tear you down. The choice does not belong to fate; it belongs to you."

By grace — despite any flaws or doubts with which I may struggle — I chose long ago, in the face of my father's suicide, to try to get better and not bitter. It has made the difference — though I must admit that as I have gotten older and continued to see so much suffering in the world, I have grown terribly weary at times.

Bitterness has not been my burden, but some other things have.

Chapter 21

ATONEMENT? — THE QUESTION OF ETERNITY

"So, the last question then becomes: Can a Christian be so depressed and temporarily blinded to the hope of the gospel that he takes his life in a temporary moment of despair? And I think the answer to that is yes ... I am waving a flag of hope that true faith can have a season that dark." — John Piper, *Desiring God: Suicide and Salvation*

Down through the years, on those rare occasions when suicide has made its way into the conversation, I have often heard someone comment with great certainty on the eternal consequences of such an act. Those who do so almost never have any idea that I lost someone to suicide, nor of the pang of emotion such pronouncements have upon me.

My guess is that whenever it is discussed in a setting where more than a few people are gathered, someone present carries the same load. The Center for Disease Control lists suicide as the tenth leading cause of death in the United States, with nearly 50,000 transpiring each year. More disturbing, well over a million suicide attempts occur annually.[15] I read somewhere that every death by suicide leaves six to eight survivors directly affected, so that is 300,000-400,000 people affected every year. A lot more people than many may imagine carry the scars and the fears of such loss. They also bear the added burden of speculation and worry about the well-being of their loved ones in the life beyond. Even those who are not especially religious often harbor such concerns.

Traditionally, all the major religions look upon suicide as spiritually unacceptable. In Hinduism, it violates the injunction against the code of non-violence; in Buddhism, against the first precept to refrain from taking a life; in Islam, against the express order, "and do not kill yourselves" found in the Quran. The vision of the consequence of suicide in such religions varies from a denial of the highest regions of blessedness, to a rebirth in a state of sadness, to a torturous existence in hell. Christianity and Judaism see this action as a violation of the commandment "You shall not kill" (Exodus 20:13), and the admonition "And for your lifeblood I will surely require a reckoning" (Genesis 9:5). In times past, Roman Catholics denied suicides a funeral mass and burial, and in Judaism, suicides have often been buried in a separate section of their cemeteries.

In recent times, mindful of the reality of mental illness, all the religions have sought to take a more sympathetic approach to the issue, but traditional mindsets have difficulty catching up with changes in official dogma. Lessons learned long ago, ingrained in both religious and social culture, have a way of sustaining themselves. Matthew Schmalz has noted that Dante's famous poem, *Inferno* (which depicted suicides consigned to the seventh level of hell as trees which painfully bleed when cut or pruned), probably did more to capture the public imagination than the official Church teachings it sought to portray.[16] I have had people from my own Baptist circles explain to me that because the last act of a suicide is a mortal sin based on a lack of faith, and since the perpetrators have no opportunity to repent and accept Christ, they have died outside the bonds of grace and are doomed to an eternity without God.

Intellectually, I rejected such teaching long ago. It makes salvation too mechanistic; makes one sin worse than all others; ignores the earnest attempts at living out a relationship with God that few, if any, of us achieve perfectly; judges the sincerity of one's claim of faith and the efficacy of the baptism that followed; and limits the reach of God's grace and the depth of God's forgiveness. If, as the teachings of my faith have attested, Jesus' death has atoned for our sins, our hope is neither found in our deeds of goodness nor lost in our misdeeds of weakness. I saw my father struggle against all that was going wrong in his life to find connection with God. I knelt in prayer beside him in worship, heard him recite the words of confession and praise in the liturgy and affirm the Apostle's Creed. I listened to him sing, with great feeling, of his love of that old rugged cross and the hope beyond this life that he found there. At the most basic level, I have put my trust for my father's eternal security in the amazing grace of a Savior whose death atoned for his sins as surely as for mine.

Yet, questions lurk. Insecurities creep in.

I have often remarked that while I affirm the doctrine of justification by faith alone, I sometimes seem to live as if my justification is found in works, that I must make my life count — and, in some weird way, not just for myself or for God, but for my father. There are times when I sense that I have subconsciously been trying to atone for my father's life and death through my own. I feel an ill-defined burden to make up for the life that he, in many ways, squandered. In her book, *Standing in the Shadow,* June Cerza Kolf asserts this may be a particular burden for "young children whose parents commit suicide (who) often feel they must overcome the stigma for the rest of their lives."[17] Some sons feel the burden of trying to live up to their father's legacy. I bear, at some subliminal level, the onus of trying to live down my father's legacy, not so much in the eyes of the world, but in the eyes of God — or maybe in my own eyes.

Such a thought is irrational and unfounded, but compelling nonetheless, prowling in some deep part of me. Whenever it comes to the surface, I remind myself of the foolishness and impossibility of trying to justify my own shortcomings, much less my father's. I reclaim my conviction that my father's hope, as well as mine, rests on the goodness of God alone, and that God understands the struggles of God's children better than we understand them ourselves.

Will I see my father again, or is he lost to me forever? That is a question I used to struggle with more than I do now, and in my struggles God sent a messenger — at least that is the way it seems to me. When I encountered the older man who worked in the funeral home — that childhood friend of my father's who told of the long-ago night at the revival when the two of them professed their faith in Jesus and then followed him in an act of baptism — he gave me a gift. He did not know it. He was just recounting a memory, but in his words I found a reassurance for which I had long searched.

Will I see my father again? If the promises of Scripture are true, I will. "For I am sure," the Apostle Paul writes in Romans, "that neither death, nor life ... nor anything else in all creation will be able to separate us from the love of God in Christ Jesus our Lord" (Romans 8:38-39). A little boy gave his heart to Jesus as best he knew how at a revival service back in the 1930s, and the Bible says nothing could ever separate him from God's love after that.

Until that day when I see for myself, I take comfort in the thought that even in the darkest season of his life when my father lost his way, his Father still looked upon him with love and compassion. In the meantime, I must learn to live with other questions.

Chapter 22

Is It Contagious? — The Question of Fear

"After all, suicide is contagious." — Suzanne Young, *The Program*

A recent Progressive Insurance ad campaign features a motivational guru whose mission is to prevent his students from becoming like their parents. The ads cleverly play upon the human propensity to behave in ways that were modeled in their formative years, and the fact that most of us are horrified to think we "are becoming our mother ... or father." Psychologists call this proclivity "imprinting." The ads are funny, but sometimes the reality is not. When you find yourself repeating the same words that used to irritate you when they came from your parents' lips, things you swore you would never say, you wonder, "Where did that come from?" You know where it came from. Imprinted patterns have a way of working their way out, even when you do not want them to.

In adulthood, one of the most troubling questions about my father's suicide for me has been, "Is it contagious?" or, to put it another way, "Whatever vulnerability was in him, is it in me?" I have always assumed and feared that whatever mental predisposition contributed to my father's suicide (and my grandfather

Willard's as well) would likely make me susceptible to the same thing. It gets in my head sometimes.

People close to me have often said that I "think too much." Situations and occurrences that others just take as they come, I tend to question and over-analyze. Is that tendency inherent? Is it somehow a reaction to the trauma of my father's death? Is that the "cloud" that settled in over my naturally sunny disposition? Is that the tendency my friend remembered when he spoke of our teenaged shenanigans, "Yeah, you did those things, but you never seemed to enjoy it like the rest of us did"?

When I described my father, I recalled that he was alternately playful and pensive. One of the greatest compliments I have cherished was from a parishioner who was a child in my first pastorate: "Brother Jim was the fun-nest preacher we ever had!" Yet, the phrase "a touch of melancholy" has also been used more than once to describe me. Playful and pensive, "fun-nest" and melancholy — do I detect a pattern here? Whenever I have been despondent, I have wondered if this is normal — or am I sinking into a depression like my father? Though I never seem to stay low for an extended time, and I have always been able to function successfully in my work and in my home life, still I wonder. Sometimes, for no discernible reason, I just go into a funk.

I went to a psychiatrist once and shared some of these concerns, told him about what was going on in my life. His assessment was that I was nowhere near clinically depressed and that I was suffering from "compassion fatigue" — taking on the burdens and problems of others and not properly finding resources and support for myself.

Once, when I was in my late forties, amid tremendous stress in my work, I had what I consider to have been a panic attack, though I am not sure the doctors ever specifically labeled it as such. Early one Sunday, I was uncontrollably emotional, weeping, unable to breathe or function, felt like I was having a heart attack. It shook me. Nothing like that had ever happened to me before, and I wondered if I was coming apart like my father did. My wife, Becky, took me to the ER. They said it was either a heart attack or a panic attack, and when all the heart tests checked out okay, I guess it left only one conclusion. They prescribed rest — a break from work. I had plenty of unused vacation time, so I took a month off — and came back to some of my most productive years of ministry.

Through all those experiences, I never seriously considered suicide a way to solve my problems. I would not want to give the impression that I have never spoken about or thought about suicide. I have, maybe too much. I think sometimes over the years I have talked too glibly about it to my wife, in times of frustration or hardship of some type, saying, "I think I just need to end it all" or "I think the world would be better off if I was out of here." I am embarrassed to recall speaking such hurtful and thoughtless words when I had absolutely no thought or intention of acting on them. I am not sure why I chose to use that particular imagery to express my anger or frustration, except that my father's action was tied to deep emotions and was also the dominant example of how someone (poorly) escaped when life's problems just became overwhelming.

Becky and I laugh sometimes about how her grandmother used to say, in such times, that she was going to just "run on down the railroad track" that bordered the back of her property where she had a garden. It was a fitting image of escape for her Depression-era generation to conjure up as an expression of their desire to flee from the problems of their lives. Granny King was not really going to run down the railroad track. She was not going anywhere. She was just frustrated, and she wanted somebody to know it. Becky's mama used that saying, and I have heard it a time or two, even though we lived nowhere near a railroad track. I wish that were the image that was passed down to me.

The only time I ever remember honestly thinking about suicide in any specific way was in the aftermath of a bout with bacterial meningitis in which I nearly died. I was hospitalized for nearly a month, most of that time in ICU. It was a harrowing and painful experience, leaving me with questions of possible neuro-logical damage, balance issues, and major hearing loss. I was on disability for six months and unsure if I would ever work again. The possibility of the loss of my health and my job, of a normal life, is the only time that I remember ever seriously contemplating whether I would prefer to end my life and how I might do it. Even then, the thought of the effect my father's actions had on those he left behind and the tarnishing of his name and memory kept such thoughts at bay. But they *were* there. And it disturbed me. Were these normal thoughts that others might have shared in a compa-rable situation, or was this a more insidious susceptibility passed on? My father had it. I had been exposed. Was it contagious?

I have become convinced that, while any act of suicide obviously involves some form of mental illness, that for my father it was acute more than chronic, and that it was exacerbated by alcoholism. If we are talking genetics, I am actually more concerned from my Grandfather Willard's lineage than my father's. The Wootens have no other suicides that I know of in their family line. My Grandfather Willard had a younger brother who took his own life in his twenties. Yet, in both their cases, alcohol played a role as well.

While I remain wary and alert, I am also convinced that they made choices that I have not made — and that I, in turn, have made choices that they did not make, and in those choices is found an altered path. I recognize a Guiding Hand bringing people into my life who have shaped a different destiny than I might otherwise have known. Though my frailties are every bit as real as any my forebears may have known, my heritage is also not without strength. I am my mother's son, as well as my father's — and in the face of unbelievable trial, devastating illness and even death itself, I never saw her wither. Colleen was fierce in her care for me and determined not to let circumstances defeat her.

In 1974, not long before my mother was diagnosed with the illness that would take her life at the tender age of forty-five, Helen Reddy recorded "You and Me Against the World," a song that always makes me think of the two of us, especially after my father's death. In it, a mother sings to her child of how the two of them together can get through anything the world throws at them, and even when one of them is no longer there, their memory will help the other carry on. It sounded just like my mother.

Strength is contagious, too!

Chapter 23

WHAT IF? — THE QUESTION OF ACCEPTANCE

Whenever people consider the big decisions that affected their lives, it is only natural to wonder what their fate may have been if a different choice was made. "What if" is an exercise most of us have undertaken at some point in our lives. We all look back and try to imagine what it would have been like if we had taken that job, or switched to a different major, or made that investment, or married that person. At a recent reunion of high school friends, one of my buddies (three or four times married, I have lost track) jokingly, or not so jokingly, said to one of the girls we used to hang out with (I do not remember his ever dating her), "I should have married you. Things would have been different." Well, it would have been different, but would it have been better?

One of my favorite movies back in the 1980s was *Peggy Sue Got Married*. Peggy Sue, a forty-three-year-old depressed mother, a housewife facing divorce, faints at her class reunion and is thrust back in time to her senior year in high school days. Armed with the knowledge of what her future was going to be like, she realizes she has the chance to rewrite her past and change her future to something "better." In the end, she finds herself making the same choices, marrying the same guy — choosing the life she lived rather than the one she imagined.

That story resonated with me, as it did with a lot of people. Who would not like to go back and fix the things that went wrong in their past? A part of me wishes that, armed with the knowledge I have now, I could go back to the past like Peggy Sue and try to take away some of my father's pain. However, the message of the movie is that we not only cannot change the past, but most of us would also not choose to do so.

While it saddens me tremendously and has haunted too many of my thoughts that my father took his own life, and though I wish his life had been happier and longer, I am not sure I would trade the life I have had for whatever life may have been had he lived. Would it have truly been better? How would his drinking and his legal entanglements have played out in my life … and in his? What would have become of my parents' relationship? Would I have flourished as much in Laurens as I did in Aiken? I would have never met my wife or had my kids, an unthinkable outcome to me. Would I have gone to college and seminary and known the life of ministry that I have known? I doubt it.

It is hard to imagine what my life would have been had he lived, but I cherish the life I have had, even with the pain of his loss. His death had a tremendous impact on me, and shaped who I have become, for better *and* for worse. The problem is — you cannot have one without the other.

This is the life I was given. I am grateful for it. And in that statement, which flows so easily from my mind as I come to the close of these pages, is found perhaps the peace which I sought when I set out to write of my father.

Life is good. It is hard, but it is good.

I wish he could have said that. I realize, maybe more than ever, how blessed I am that I can.

*The Wooten family today: (front row) Jim and Becky,
with granddaughter Avery Wooten; (back row) Spencer
and Lee Ann Wooten Watson, Grant and Ashley Wooten.
(Photo by Meredith Murray)*

Epilogue

Following Jim's death, Colleen had a couple of "gentlemen callers" who came courting. One of them was a divorcee a couple of years younger than she. In August of 1963, she married Jim Beane and we moved to Aiken, South Carolina, where she continued her career in the savings and loan business and I flourished with new friends and new opportunities. Aiken was a good place to grow up as I entered my teenage years, and in many ways we left behind some of the associations with my father's life and death. However, early on, in November of 1963, Colleen contracted uterine cancer and almost died. It was a frightening time in my life, but thankfully after surgery and a lengthy hospitalization, she recovered. She told me she prayed that the Lord would let her see me grow up. That was her greatest concern.

My stepfather's roots (as well as ours) were in Laurens, so especially in the early years of their marriage we returned often on the weekends and holidays for gatherings with his four older sisters and their families, and to visit Granny. The Beane family was close and made Mama and me both feel welcomed. I would also visit Mother Renee and the Wooten clan on many of the trips, but as I got older and more involved in sports and social activities in Aiken, my trips to Laurens became much less frequent.

In March of 1969 (my junior year in high school), we moved again — much to my dismay — to Greenville. Mama continued her career with the savings and loan. It turned out to be the best move of my life, but at the time I resented being uprooted from the identity I had carved out in Aiken. My new school was the largest in the state, and with only a little over a year left, I was not sure if I could find my place, with new friendships and an identity of my own. I did. Instead of student government and football, as before, I immersed myself into dramatics. I was cast in the lead role in the first play of my senior year, *The Rainmaker.* From that experience, I was recruited for the lead in an original play that won the competition in the state drama festival, and, more importantly, won the heart of the girl who played my girlfriend. Becky and I have been married since 1973, and any good I have known or done in this world, I credit to her. We have a son, Grant, who is a chemical engineer, and a daughter, Lee Ann, who is an attorney. So far, we have one granddaughter, Avery.

I wish so much my parents could have known my children. That is the shape of the grief of my adulthood. Colleen died at the age of forty-five in 1975, one month after I was called to my first pastorate while a seminary student in Kentucky. Doctors said that transfusions she had received during her cancer treatment were likely tainted with hepatitis which, by the time it was discovered, had done irreversible damage. She fought with stoicism and dignity for nine months before she lost the battle. I suppose her prayer to see me grow up was answered, but I wish she could have shared so much more of my life.

I have written of how I longed for someone to talk to me about the events of the past. In fairness, I believe she wanted to do so in those closing months of her life. In my emotional immaturity and denial of the finality of her illness, I was the one who turned the conversation to something else whenever she broached anything that seemed like "words before I die." On my trips home from Kentucky when she would be sick or hospitalized, she always rallied remarkably. I convinced myself she would continue to do so. Against all reason, I was shocked when, after one of her rallies, I returned to Kentucky only to get a call almost immediately upon arrival that she had died. She was buried in the Forest Lawn Cemetery in Laurens among my stepfather's family, not far from Carlton's grave in one section and the one where Granny would be buried in another.

The others in the story passed from the scene in the intervening years, most relatively soon after she did: my Aunt Mary and Uncle Grant, later Mother Renee, eventually Aunt Martha. Papa had died not long after Daddy. All of them are buried on that hill near my father in the Laurens Cemetery. Of the six cousins, only Renee and I are left. I often ponder with sadness the way the burial places reflect the dysfunction of my family, the brokenness of the relationships in those who shaped my life. My father lies in one cemetery, with an empty plot beside him, his siblings and parents nearby. My mother rests four miles away, with an empty plot beside her, surrounded by my stepfather's family, while he, after remarrying, was buried in Greenville. Carlton and Granny are not far from my mother, but not together. Sometimes, I contemplate relocating somebody, as if that will fix things in death that could not be fixed in life. I cannot figure out how to do it. I never could.

After forty-four years of serving as a pastor in five different churches, I retired in 2019 — with the hope of spending time with my family, traveling the world, and finally putting pen to paper on the ideas and stories that have rattled around in my brain over the years. It is this story that has cried out to be written first, before I could move on to other projects. I hope somebody is reading it now and maybe finding some meaning in it, but I had to write it whether anyone much reads it or not. For my own sanity, I had to give some order to the flittering memories and baffling questions that pop up willy-nilly in my mind, to try to make some sense of it all.

My quest led me back to Laurens, checking police reports and coroner's records, researching newspaper accounts, and revisiting the places where once we all had lived out both the mundane as well as dramatic moments of my formative years. I wanted to test what facts I could find against my recollections and to fill in the blanks as best I could.

In the process, the most amazing thing occurred. I contacted Jim Coleman, the county auditor, a friend who had been a member of the church I served there nearly forty years ago. I had the names of all the pallbearers and honorary pallbearers listed in the newspaper article I found at the library. They would all be in their nineties, and I presumed all were deceased. Jim confirmed my suspicions.

We went to lunch and met up with some other old acquaintances. As we ate, I told them of my project. (As I think on it now, when I mentioned my father's suicide, I whispered when I got to "that word" — and they all were mute, stone-faced. The stigma and the discomfort are still there, apparently for me, as well as others.) I mentioned a childhood friend named Jim Watson (a lot of us were named Jim back then, it seems) who I thought could help me clear up a sequence of events that I could not quite get to fit. One of the diners, David Coggins, another former church friend who knows everybody in Laurens, said, "I got his cell phone number right here."

I called Jim Watson right then, and he invited me to come on out to see him. He shared vivid memories of my father. He spoke of how he mainly remembered about my mother that she was pretty, and of how he thinks he spent the night at our house right before my father's death. He told me of how upset his parents were when it happened, but how they never discussed or specu- lated about his death with their children. In the conversation, he mentioned a couple who were friends with his parents and mine. I remembered them well. She was my mother's best friend years ago. He said, "They are still living — ninety-two and ninety-five years old — and both are sharp." He gave me their phone number.

I thought I had waited too late, that all I had were my memories, that anyone who really knew my father and mother when these events unfolded was gone. Here were two people who knew them since before they dated, remembered when I was born, went on vacations with us — and they lived not ten minutes from where I did. It was a gift to find them. Primarily, they confirmed my recol- lection, gave me confidence in the accuracy of my memory — but they also solved a mystery or two and awakened some other memories. Mostly, they made my parents live again. Through their words, I could see my parents — dancing at Curry's Lake, walking to the old post office, standing in the kitchen, vacationing at the beach, working at the radio station, playing pranks I never heard about before, and on and on.

These old friends confirmed a suspicion or two; they corrected a misconception or two. They knew some details about my father's death that I did not know, the most compelling of which were both the identity of his girlfriend and the firsthand report from the police chief that she had received the late-night call from my father in which he threatened suicide if she would not leave town with him. Still, ultimately they, like everyone else, were left with unanswered questions and mere speculations. Such is the nature of suicide.

But I am good, as least for now. Somebody who was there finally talked to me.

And not just my parents' friends. The words of that childhood friend, Jim Watson, stay with me. When he asked about the book I was writing about my father's death, I said, "I've known the title for a long time: *The Suicide's Son*. That's who I am." He interrupted, "That's not how I see you! I don't even think about that when I remember you."

I find some comfort in that thought. My father's actions do not define me, even in the eyes of those who knew me then. I may be the Suicide's Son, but there is more to me than that.

All of us are shaped by our parents' actions, for good or bad. None of us are defined by them.

Our lives are what we make of them.

END NOTES

1. Lauren Oliver, *Delirium* (New York: Harper Collins, 2011), pp. 10-11.

2. Kay Redfield Jamison, *Night Falls Fast: Understanding Suicide, 1st edition* (New York: Alfred A. Knopf, 1999), p. 73.

3. Earl Wooten lost his major league baseball position because (in typical Wooten fashion) he flashed an independent streak. After being called up to the big leagues and batting .256 in 1948, the Senators wanted him to refrain from playing basketball during the off-season and focus on gaining weight and strength to get ready for spring training. Earl loved basketball and continued to play in the Textile leagues (under an assumed name, I was told, until he was inevitably "found out"). The Senators sold his contract to the Boston Braves, who assigned him to their AAA team, where he remained from 1949-1955. Despite leading the league with a .346 batting average and making the All-Star team in 1955, he was never called up to the "bigs" again and retired in 1955. [John Chandler Griffin, *Moments of Glory: South Carolina's Greatest Sports Heroes 1913-1977* (Columbia: Summerhouse Press, 1997), pp. 64-65.]

4. An article about that golden age of sports published in January of 2021 said, "The textile league had stars of its own, with Earl Wooten taking top billing, the former players and coaches say." It quoted two old-timers who played against him, Eddie Cannon and "Fig" Newton. "Earl Wooten from Pelzer," Cannon said. "I remember, he'd go down in the corner and shoot hook shots and never miss. He was good." Added Newton, "I used to try to guard him all the time. With the best I got, I held him to 40 one time." [https://livingupstatesc.com/southern-textile-league-basketball-was-upstates-march-madness-for-more-than-50-years.]

At just 5'11", Wooten shined in baseball, football and basketball. Despite college scholarship offers, he went to work in Pelzer's textile mill, retiring from J.P. Stevens, where he was athletic director. Wooten, who died in 2006 at the age of eighty-two, is a member of the South Carolina Athletic Hall of Fame in basketball and baseball.

5. David Duncan Wallace, *The Life of Henry Laurens* (New York: G.P. Putnam's Sons, The Knickerbocker Press, 1915), pp. 389-411.

6. Tyler Perry, *Don't Make a Black Woman Take Off Her Earrings: Madea's Uninhibited Commentaries on Love and Life* (New York: Riverhead Books, 2007), p. 3.

7. I am fairly certain the older one, the brash big-talker, got the harsher judgment, befitting the instigator. I did find records that showed he continued to struggle personally and financially, with divorces and bankruptcies before dying in Tennessee at age sixty-eight. His daughter wrote: "Dad, there's not a lot I can say. I really never got to know you. A person has to learn to forgive. I thank God He showed me how. Maybe we will get another chance." The younger also divorced (while in prison) but remarried and seems to have had a more settled and conventional life. He remained in South Carolina until his death at the age of eighty-five.

8. Carla Fine, *No Time to Say Goodbye* (New York: Doubleday, 1997), p. 68.

9. Mariel Hemingway, *Out Came the Sun: Overcoming the Legacy of Mental Illness, Addiction, and Suicide in my Family* (New York: Regan Arts, 2015), p. 234.

10. Jamison, *Night Falls*, p. 18.

11. Jamison, *Night Falls*, pp. 276-277.

12. https://www.knowyourquotes.com/When-We-Played-Softball-Id-Steal-Second-Base-Feel-Guilty-And-Go-Back-Woody-Allen.html.

13. Jamison, *Night Falls*, p. 85.

14. Orson Scott Card, *Ender's Shadow* (New York: Tom Doherty Associates, 1999), p. 237.

15. https://www.cdc.gov/suicide/index.html.

16. Matthew Schmalz, "Why Religions of the World Condemn Suicide," theconversation.com, June 12, 2018.

17. June Cerza Kolf, *Standing in the Shadow: Help and Encouragement for Suicide Survivors* (Grand Rapids: Baker Books, 2002), p. 40.

Additional sources, not previously noted in the text:

https://www.quotes.net/quote/18508
(Alan Valentine quote on p. v)

https://www.goodreads.com/quotes
(Umar Ibn Al-Khattaab quote on p. 127)

www.deepakchopra.com/articles/some-truth-about-you/
(Deepak Chopra quote on p. 131)

https://www.goodreads.com/quotes
(Josh Shipp quote on p. 141)

CPSIA information can be obtained
at www.ICGtesting.com
Printed in the USA
LVHW080842101221
705841LV00015B/809/J